A gift from Amazo
Get access to the B(
Novel series o.

Make sure to bookmark the bonus materials web page as we ͟ ͟ ͟er-ring to it throughout the series

INCLUDES:

- ✓ Four Part Story Structure Scrivener Starter File
- ✓ Four Part Story Structure MS Word Starter File
- ✓ FREE and $0.99 Submission Site List
- ✓ *Nine Day Novel: Self-Editing* Bonus Videos
- ✓ Outlining Example Beat Sheet Scrivener File

To get access to the bonuses Click HERE or visit

vixenink.com

NINE DAY NOVEL

OUTLINING

THE BASICS

STEVE WINDSOR

Published by

vixenink.com

::Disclaimer

This book is for informational purposes only.

The information found within the contents of this book may contain third-party products and services. These third-party materials consist of products and opinions expressed by their owners. As such, the author and/or the publisher do not assume responsibility or liability for any third-party material or opinions expressed.

The use of recommended third-party material does not guarantee any success and/or earnings related to you or your business. Publication of such third-party material is simply a recommendation and an expression of the author's own opinion of that particular material.

Links to third-party resources may be affiliate links, meaning the author may receive compensation if a service is ultimately purchased from such a link.

VIXEN ink

Although the author and publisher have made every effort to ensure that the information in this book was correct at press time, the author and publisher do not assume and hereby disclaim any liability to any party for any loss, damage, or disruption caused by errors or omissions, whether such errors or omissions result from negligence, accident, or any other cause.

NINE DAY NOVEL: OUTLINING

A VIXEN ink book/Published by arrangement with the author

Copyright © 2015 by Steve Windsor

Cover design by:

Steve Windsor - book cover design

vixenink.com/book-covers/

All rights reserved.

No part of this book may be reproduced, scanned, or distributed in any printed or electronic form without permission

ISBN-13: 978-1511732451
ISBN-10: 1511732458

Dedication

To you as you start your journey to becoming a published author.

TABLE OF CONTENTS

COVER	i
BONUS MATERIALS	ii
Title Page	iii
Disclaimer	iv
Copyright	v
Dedication	vi
TABLE OF CONTENTS	vii
Introduction	3
BONUSES	15
Why Bother Outlining?	17
Inspiration	21
Your Own Story	31
Story Concept	35
Themes	43
Settings and Vocabulary	51
Research	59
Characters	63
Story Summaries	89
Beat Sheet Outline	99
Example 4PSS Outline	119
About the Author	179

NINE DAY NOVEL: OUTLINING

1
INTRODUCTION

SO YOU WANT TO WRITE A NOVEL?

You have dreams of traveling the road to riches, following the likes of Stephen King, Danielle Steel, George RR Martin. . . Maybe you even wanna be the next Tolstoy!

I think we've all had those feelings when we first entertained the idea that writing could be more than a wish, a dream, or a precious fantasy we had one day. I know I did.

No more overbearing, micromanaging bosses and no more two-hour time-wasting commutes, stuck in traffic with 100,000 other employees, trudging our way to our horrible jobs. I'd just outsource all that pesky life minutiae and seclude myself on my own private island and write on the beach all day. Right?

Welcome to Fantasy Island.

I knew that island was out there . . . somewhere. Everything I'd ever dreamt, just bobbing in the ocean all warm and happily ever after—my fuchsia Adirondack beach chair, basking in the sun with a Piña Colada resting on its left arm . . . waiting for me. (If you're gonna have a dream, you might as well make it specific!)

The trouble? I had no idea where that island was located. And I wondered. . . If I only had some idea how to get there. A road map to write my way to fame and fortune . . . forevermore. I needed a direction to travel—some destination that I knew existed. Then I could simply take the first step towards it and every step after would bring me closer to the end—my goal. A satisfying end to a hard-fought journey.

Sound like the beginning of a bad motivational book? Maybe. . . Or maybe it's a great analogy. Because maybe all you and I need to start that entire journey—take that first step and write that first word of your novel—is a map!

This book is your map.

Funny things, maps. Nowadays, we've gotten so accustomed to full-time satellite, GPS tracking systems at the tips of our fingers, heads-up displays in our cars, and palm-held devices that can locate us to within 10 feet on the planet . . . that we've forgotten how they actually work.

Now, when faced with the task of drawing one up for

ourselves—making a road map for our novel and our hero to follow on their quest to redemption, revenge, romance or wraith removal. . . Well, many of us just start writing in any old direction without a clue of whether or not we're getting any closer, let alone an idea of where our hero needs to end up. (They call those people "pantsers." We'll get back to them.)

An outline helps.

We need a map . . . to teach us how to create a map . . . for our hero's journey. And that's why I wrote this book. Because an outline for your novel is exactly that—a map that you'll use to write your hero through his journey to the end.

Your hero is at point A (opening scene) and you want him or her to arrive at point Z (the new equilibrium) . . . in a fantastic and fun fashion. Along the way, you want him or her to pass by points B through Y, barely making it to Z. It's really that simple. (Wink-wink—nothing ever is.)

But the way you're going to learn how to outline is the same way experts in every profession get that way— repetition, repetition. I'll show you story-outlining techniques so many different ways that it'll seem redundant at first. That is, until you realize that **all of the different methods authors use to outline and plot their novels** are actually just variations of four simple parts.

THIS IS A HOW-TO BOOK

If you've read any of the other books in this *Nine Day Novel* series, you know that I like to get down to business and talk about the reality of writing physical words. Put the "how" back in how-to. Because motivation, muse, and "mushery" are not my strong suits.

I know how to motivate myself, inspiration is screaming all around me and I've taught myself to listen to it. As for "mushery," I just made that word up as a catch-all phrase for every esoteric, ethereal, evangelical, emotionally "educating" book I've ever read on writing. Because at the end of every one of those pieces of "inner-journey" advice, I've always been left staring at the pages saying, "Yeah, yeah, but what do I do? Where do I start?"

START HERE

If you want to learn about:

- Getting ideas for a novel
- Creating plots that people care about
- Finding inspiration in everyday life
- Weaving your own journey into your novel's plot

- High-concept storytelling
- The difference between plotting and "pantsing"
- The way I prefer to outline my novels
- Why you shouldn't care one bit about my "method"

And at the end of it, I'll show you a step-by-step format that you can use to outline your novel. Add it to your tool kit . . . or just use pieces of it to improve your own methods. Outlining is like writing—use what everyone else does to find your own style.

Darth, you're a sarcastic slave driver!

MY WRITER "VOICE"

That last statement is as good a time as any to introduce you to my "writer voice."

In *Nine Day Novel: Writing*, I talked about some hardcore, probably uncomfortable "methods" that I use to pump words onto the page like precious blood spilled on a battlefield. I don't mince words, I pound the keyboard and force the words out. That's just how I am. I realize that everyone learns and lives and loves to write differently. I just prefer things hard, hot and heavy. (That didn't sound right.)

Anyway, it was in the spirit of raw hard work that this series has taken shape as a "Darth Vader"-style kick in the butt to my fellow writer peeps. Authors who are struggling with wading through the often daunting task of outlining, writing, editing, self-publishing, and marketing their first novel.

THERE IS NO MAGIC

I make no qualms in showing you that the task of writing a novel isn't the Master of Arts rocket science magic that your English literature professor makes it out to be. Writing is creative art, to be sure, but that creation is a learnable skill and isn't bestowed by universities as a divine right only attainable by the few who are deemed worthy. Moreover, it's spilled forth from a billion different souls with a billion different styles and a billion different reasons for doing it. No one "way" is the way and no one person can tell you yours.

Study hard, learn hard, write hard. Dedicate yourself and do the hard work. That's what writing requires of you. And that's what I'm here to help you do.

Writing is a muscle.

Writing's no different from lifting weights or learning to

drive a car or learning how to cook. Precious few birth straight from the womb with a barbell, spatula or quill pen in their hand, begging for a notepad so they can get all of those amazing words they were born with, captured and onto the page.

And when those "gifted" few do birth right from the womb, they oftentimes dole out advice that dissuades, discourages and destroys the rest of us mere mortals' collective wills to write. My commitment to you is to prevent that from happening!

Most of writing is hard work and like anything else, the more of it you do, the better you get at it. So, as your momentary mentor, "Darth Vader," occasionally in my books, I . . . "encourage" you to stop worrying about whether you've been "gifted" with the ability to write, and simply get going growing that "gift" by "doing the Darth"—sucking it up and getting down and dirty with the hard work.

Enough said. Let's get to it!

THE "WISK" SECTION

It can be said by more than a few that I'm a "cheeky" bastard. That is true. It's also true that I'm a cuddly, snuggly teddy bear on the inside. Way . . . down . . . deep . . .

on the inside. For that reason, and because I'd read enough quotes from people about the master Stephen King's words of wisdom, I decided to create my own quote section for my own books.

At the beginning of most chapters, instead of a pithy quote you've heard or read a million times—"show don't tell" or some other piece of "helpful" parable of pontification—you'll get a completely new and maybe semi-naughty little tidbit from yours truly. It's just part of the value.

WISK—The "When I'm Stephen King" section

I LIKE TO HAVE SOME FUN.

The subject of writing can get dry. I like to hose it down every once in a while with some wet and wild observations. My hope is that a little humor helps you process, understand and store all this information. What was that *Mary Poppins* song? Oh yeah, "A spoonful of sugar . . . helps the medicine go down . . . the medicine go down. . ."

I know, right? Darth Vader and Mary Poppins together—totally crazy! Mary Poppins with a lightsaber! Now that's a high-concept story! We'll talk about that in a bit.

"Now," in the immortal words of Johnny Depp in *Rango*, "we ride!"

MY WRITING PARTNER

Lise Cartwright is my writing buddy and fast becoming my dear friend, though I've never met her. She lives in New Zealand and I'm in the U.S. and we collaborate over the Internet. Lise is a long-time freelance writer and very successful non-fiction author. I'm closing in fast on her heels in non-fiction.

I mention this because I'm preparing to bring her up to speed on fiction storytelling using this book to outline a novel we're going to co-author. It'll be a blast!

OUR OWN LITTLE STORY

In the previous *Nine Day Novel* books, many of you said that overlaying the stories as examples on top of the Four Part Story Structure was the most helpful part of those books. So, continuing with the "don't fix what ain't broke" daddy-ism my father taught me, *Dixxon—Teen Witch* will be the example novella that I refer to throughout this book.

This next project has me taking a break from *The Fallen* series of dystopian religious thrillers that I write, and has

Lise and me co-authoring this novella called *Dixxon*. We're using this *Nine Day Novel: Outlining* book as a practical application road map to help us actually outline that series and story. Then we're going to write it in real time together using online document collaboration tools like Google Docs or Evernote.

It's going to be a lot of fun. This book will make that possible. Because on the very first day of our "nine-day" novella, we're going to use *NDN: Outlining* to structure the entire book, plotting the first *Dixxon* story using the Four Part Story Structure (4PSS).

FOUR PART STORY STRUCTURE

The 4PSS was popularized by Larry Brooks in his book, *Story Engineering*. I broke it down for you in rabbit-punching detail in my book, *Nine Day Novel: Writing*. In the last section of this book, I'll do that again, inserting our *Dixxon* novella milestones as an example case.

In short, Lise and I are using this outlining book to outline *Dixxon* using the Four Part Story Structure milestones.

"How" in how-to. That's what I promised, right?

Cut to Darth—

I slide my hand along my black leather belt, slithering my fingers towards my lightsaber. My thumb rubs gently over the power selector. Is it time yet? Are they paying attention? I relax my hand. We'll see . . . we'll see.

:: ACTION ITEM

If you haven't yet, I shamelessly suggest that you review my *Nine Day Novel: Writing* book to get an in-depth understanding of the Four Part Story Structure. If you're comfortable with it, move on. If not, and you just want to get to it, here's a down and dirty—quick look—at the Four Part Story Structure that will help this book make more sense.

4PSS Quick Start

A million different stories are told using a format as old as Aristotle—Four Part Story Structure. Many different "methods" have been developed to describe it, but the basics are found in four parts. (Movie writers call it three-act structure, but there are four parts to the story.)

1 - Setup - opening scenes, killer hook, inciting incident
2 - Reaction - run for your life, figure out what you're up against
3 - Resolve - turn and fight back and lose, the hero's world changes again

4 - Climax - hero accepts reality, final battle scene, new equilibrium (ride into the sunset).

Totally simple.

2
BONUSES

INCLUDED BONUSES

I wanted to make the *Nine Day Novel* series bonuses as valuable, if not more valuable, than the books themselves. I've packed in things like a Four Part Story Structure Scrivener starter file, self-editing tutorial videos and more.

And since all of the bonuses in the series are cumulative, if you've bought one book and signed up to get access to them, then you have access to all of the bonuses.

For this book, the bonus is going to be a more detailed Scrivener starter file of the Four Part Story Structure as a .scriv file. It'll be an outline beat sheet example that you can follow and fill out and replace—a guide to help you brainstorm, concept, outline and plot your novel right inside Scrivener.

The two videos that Lise and I recorded as we brainstormed the entire outline for *Dixxon—Teen Witch*, in just over three hours, will be on the bonuses' web page. We both loved it! They're a good view into how the "sausage" is made and will give you a little idea as to how brainstorming for ideas really works. Get a cup of coffee or tea because the videos are pretty long.

:: ACTION ITEM

Take a minute to get access to all of the bonus materials for the *Nine Day Novel* series.

You can get access to them by clicking HERE or going to vixenink.com and signing up for author updates.

3
WHY BOTHER OUTLINING?

WISK

"If you're gonna spend 90 hours trying to write a novel . . . it might be nice to know where you're headed."

Or. . .

"I can drag you to the outlining well, but you'll have to decide whether or not to drink the Four Part Story Structure water."

Everything's optional.

Outlining isn't mandatory—it's not for everyone. "Pantsers" (remember them?) are authors who write by the seat of their pants, so to speak—make it up as they go along. They don't normally outline, but many end up meandering their way to story structure anyway.

Here are some advantages to outlining over pantsing.

Saving time

By planning out your story, you'll cut down on the amount of time you spend writing your novel. Think of your outline's plot points and milestones as rocks sticking out of a pond full of alligators. You can hop from point to point, crossing the pond unscathed, but if you fall off—follow your characters sideways in your story—at the very least you'll get delayed. Worse, you might never make it back to your tale alive!

Spotting story problems

Since outlining gives you a broader and higher-level perspective of your story, you can spot story problems, potential pitfalls and plot holes before they happen.

If you're a pantser, you might paint yourself into a plot corner. At the very least, you'll have to paint yourself back out again, wasting time and effort. Outlining can help avoid that.

Brainstorming for ideas

Getting your mind fired up for your story by mapping it out beforehand, helps you get clear about what story you're telling. I can tell you, that by doing that very thing for *Dixxon* as I wrote this book, I could probably write the story without ever looking at my outline—I've outlined it so many ways that the story is ingrained in my memory before I've written it.

Foreshadowing

Outlining helps you strategically place information in your story as you go, foreshadowing future events. By knowing where you're going in the progression of your story, future mysteries can be alluded to and "hidden" earlier in your plot to provide an added layer of enjoyment and entertainment for your reader.

However you look at it, I'm a big fan of outlining your story before you start. Even if you only use your outline as a guide and choose to never look at it again—as I've said—at least you'll have a much better idea of where your story is headed before you ever start.

4
INSPIRATION

WISK

"Pay attention to your surroundings. They're the cheapest inspiration you can buy."

INSPIRATION VS. PERSPIRATION

I took the review comments from *Nine Day Novel: Writing* and *Nine Day Novel: Self-Editing* to heart. One of them asked about inspiration and brainstorming and the concept and feeling that I mentioned earlier. In answer to that, it's my belief that inspiration is all around us, buried quite shallowly for that matter. What there's a precious lack of, is the supply of perspiration that many authors are willing to expend in order to dig it up.

Here's some examples of where you can find inspiration.

Murder mystery writer? Read the newspaper.

A newspaper is a quaint and outdated method of information delivery, but thankfully available in digital format right next to the ebook you're most likely reading right now. Take any news headline and use that for the basis of your next fiction plot.

Example:

Recently, a headline I saw read, "San Francisco police find suitcase filled with dismembered body parts." (Seriously, you don't have to make this stuff up.) If you're a murder mystery writer, that should set your brain off on a million different scenarios and stories for how that poor soul ended up in that suitcase.

To date, I don't believe I've seen a follow-up story that found the police solving the "dismembered man" mystery thriller.

Heartfelt emotional writer? Observe everyday life.

I'm serious about this. Most people aren't paying close attention to their surroundings. The constant assault of marketing information and minutiae overload have caused many of us to develop a defense mechanism called "selective cognizant thought." (Okay, I made that up. Sounded cool though.) But it's true—we filter. If we didn't, all that email and information would drown us.

:: ACTION ITEM

The next time you're stuck trying to find your next novel idea, go to your favorite coffeehouse, get a cup of your most delicious writing "inspiration" and pretend to write on your computer. Then listen and watch . . . carefully.

Example:

Here's what happened to me when I did this. (Yes, technically it's eavesdropping and some people are offended by that, but don't get me—don't make me get my lightsaber out. Focus!)

Anyway, there's a gaggle of regulars at my beloved Peets coffeehouse, and one particular group is in their late 70s for sure. They meet often. About six of them, men and women. And do you want to know what they talk about? Well, it's not gardens and grandkids, nor is it aches and pains and prescriptions, I can assure you.

They talk about sex. I'm not kidding you. Vegas vacations of old and strippers with big breasts and how they remember when one of them in the group went off in an alley. . . I'm not gonna elaborate, but I got seriously off my word count one day, because I just had to listen to them.

And it's not just the men, as you might suspect. The women are as bad or, depending on your perspective, as deliciously devious as the men. And none of them cares who hears them, or they've just lost that much hearing in their old age that they speak louder than many around them are comfortable hearing. (I know it's not that uncommon, but most of us don't think that way about anyone older than us. I actually ended up talking to them and having a good laugh about it.)

I found their entire conversation wonderfully fascinating and also idea-inspiring to the point of distracting me from the project I was on. In fact, I've named their generational romance novel that I've half-written in my head "Coffee Club." Their journey through life and love and concubines and conquest, finally settling in for their golden years, looking back and finding peace and purpose in everything from the prostitutes to the pompous—the randomness of the insanity called life.

Science-fiction writer? Prepare to perspire.

Science-fiction writing can be as easy as making it all up yourself, or it can be as hard as researching technology that could plausibly exist in the world you want to create.

Sci-fi is one big "what if?"

Nowhere is this more important than in sci-fi. After all, have you ever been in space? Unless you're one of the handful of astronauts who have, you're most likely going to have to make all that stuff up. Thankfully, that's not really the case.

The reason being, most of the hard work of sci-fi has been done for you. Spaceports, space marines, aliens, weightlessness, communicators, weapons, starships. . . The list is insanely endless and sci-fi fans love and take their fandom to a level of seriousness that borders on . . . well, downright reality.

Most of the technology that you use to communicate and create with each day was pure science fiction 50 years ago. And none of it would exist if it hadn't been for one fictitious person—James Tiberius Kirk.

That's right, I said it. And dare I say that James T. Kirk would kick Darth Vader's black helmet senseless! But what he would also do—did—is inspire an entire generation of 70s and 80s youth to grow up and invent things like cell phones and the Internet and global positioning systems.

Stop worrying if you're different enough and start improving on what's already great.

Heaven help us when they finally perfect the transporter. I'm not worried though—Jeff Goldblum in The *Fly* pretty much doused the supply of volunteers to test it.

And those rabid sci-fi fans—I can you tell I'm one of them—love their genre as much as they love the technology in it.

The point is that the information in sci-fi is all around you as well. You need only watch the shows and read the books in that genre to find examples of what you're looking for. For that matter, look around the house and picture yourself being transported here from the 1940s. Can you imagine? Your toaster is space-age sci-fi. And from when I started working in technology, your cell phone has more power than the $5,000 computers we were buying to run entire companies!

Project yourself into the future and re-imagine what technologies we will have invented to help ourselves do even less work. Books that write themselves. Wouldn't that be nice?

Help me out here, Darth.

I reach for my lightsaber, seeing if they've taken the bait. Maybe. . . They're learning—the hard work is the point. Books that write themselves? What fun would that be?

Make it up as you go along.

The beauty is that after you do that hard work, the sky (no pun) is the limit. Because no one knows what's out there in space or even whether or not aliens exist, so you're free to let your mind run wild with possibilities.

Read *Popular Science* or *WIRED* magazine to find new and crazy technologies being invented. Scour the Internet for those same technological breakthroughs. Watch the news to keep pace on drones and spying and mini-cameras and artificial intelligence the government is using. . . Uh-oh. I almost got off on a conspiracy rant. Whew.

Example:

Better yet, watch the reality of what multi-gazillionnaires, like Virgin executive Richard Branson, are doing in the race to commercialize outer space for profit.

Imagine a dystopian world where the poor are left down on Earth to fend for themselves in the sweltering cesspool of crime and pollution that the wealthy created. Meanwhile, those same rich people live on beautiful orbiting greenhouses, far above the atmosphere and the dangers down on Earth.

Uh-oh, the movie *Elysium*—Matt Damon—already did that.

A PICTURE IS WORTH A THOUSAND WORDS . . . OF INSPIRATION

In our author world, a picture may be worth a whole lot more than that. In fact, it might just inspire the 50,000-100,000 words in your next novel. Here's what I mean:

I'm a bit of a Photoshop freak. I design my own book covers and work with other authors to design theirs. Shameless plug for my services aside, a book cover—image—can inspire the entire world, theme, plot, character or your hero, and all the other ideas for your next novel.

Our own little story

The idea for our novella, *Dixxon*, started with a conversation about Lise's niece. Shortly after, I did what I always do—headed to stock photography sites to see if I could find an image that inspired the rest of it. The image I found was awesome and gave us both the jumpstart for our hero and her entire teen witch world. You can see it as it's the cover for our novella example in this book.

:: ACTION ITEM

You don't have to be a book cover designer to make this strategy work for you. The next time you want to find inspiration for a particular genre that you'd like to write about, head over to popular stock photography sites like shutterstock, istockphoto, or better yet for us independent authors on a budget, dollarphotoclub.

Writing a romance? Simply search for that very term on the stock photo site of your choice. Want to write a mystery about a woman? Search for "mystery woman." Whatever you're interested in writing, simply search that genre or term. The hard part will be perusing the pages and pages of images that aren't so awesome in order to find the one gem that speaks to you—"inspires" your world.

One of the coolest searches on stock photo sites is "mysterious." It returns some of the most creative and awesome images. In fact, if you pay close attention, you'll see a bunch of photos you recognize as indie author book covers.

Yours is in there . . . somewhere.

5
YOUR OWN STORY

WISK
"You want to find a hero? Look in the mirror."

Be your own hero.

There's a common piece of advice that floats around out there in the author advice-o-sphere, and that is: Don't use your own life as the basis for your story. While it may be that we authors have a skewed belief that our own experiences will make for good fiction, that doesn't mean that we can't draw on our lives, areas of expertise, struggles, triumphs, loves and losses to give authenticity and believability to our stories.

In fact, for your very first novel, your own life's struggles may be just the stick of dynamite you'll need to break free from the logjam of doubt, hesitation and procrastination that's stopped you from starting and finishing your story in the first place.

Your first novel may suck. Write it anyway.

Will your life story be compelling? Will you become an internationally acclaimed author whose novels are celebrated alongside *Harry Potter, Lord of the Rings* and *Game of Thrones?* Or will you pen the next insane 50 shades of erotica? Chances are high that the answer is no. But, as you know from my other books in the *Nine Day Novel* series, the purpose of your first novel is not to make you rich. Its purpose is practice and growth and creating writing habits and gathering and growing the skills you'll need in order to write a better book the next time.

So, if tightly weaving in your own life's experiences gets that first novel job done faster. . . If you get your first completed draft under your belt by staying close to your own story, just do it. Don't put the pressure of success on your first effort. Put the words on the paper—do the hard work. After all, the hero's journey is your own story as an author. It is—in fact. . .

The Four Part Story Structure of your own author journey.

In **Part 1** you're minding your own business, barely thinking about writing or just trying to put that crazy dream out of your mind. Something snaps and you decide that you have to become an author—inciting incident.

Then in **Part 2** you run for your life, wandering aimlessly with no idea what being a professional writer is all about. You struggle and strive and flail around with no help and no progress. In short, you're lost. But by the time you reach the end of Part 2—through trial and tribulation and failure—you understand what you're up against as an independent author. And that revelation is that writing is Darth-Vader hard work.

In **Part 3** of your author journey, you vow to succeed— you turn to fight, win the damsel, woo the boyfriend or defeat the bad guys. Your first novel is crap, because that's its job—being crappy. You learn, you grow and you write another one, because you're gonna win, dammit!

But success is elusive and slow. So you seek help and find information and assistance in other authors on your same journey. Then you find the key—persevere, learn, practice, write, rinse, repeat.

In **Part 4**, armed with that hard-won knowledge and skill, you do battle with yourself, with the critics, and with the hard work, and you finally, painstakingly . . . win. You publish a book. Maybe it's your third one or fourth or fifth —who knows? What you do know is that your first successful book wouldn't have been possible had you never finished that first one. And at the end of it all, you ride into the sunset victorious—an author.

What better story of "overnight" success is there than that?

:: ACTION ITEM

I rarely sideline to motivational mushery, but let's try it out. Take a few minutes and outline a fictitious autobiography for yourself. About your journey as an author. Answer these questions:

Part 1 - What was your life like before you decided to write? What caused you to finally write?

Part 2 - What early struggles did you have as you started to write?

Part 3 - What happened the time that you almost gave up and called it quits?

Part 4 - You may not be here yet, so make it up, because you're a fiction writer, remember, but what does your life look like now that you've fought your way to being a successful author? Do you live on an island next to mine?

Welcome neighbor.

6
STORY CONCEPT

WISK

"Help me, Obi-Wan Kenobi, you're my only hope." Okay that's some nostalgic Princess Leia in Star Wars, however. . .

Cry all you want to for help, you're still going to have to learn and understand the following things: high concept, theme, story structure, and characters.

Here's my version of the above quote:

"Oh, Darth, I just can't do this—my lightsaber's too heavy!"
"Grow stronger."

The good news in all this is that if you read *Nine Day Novel: Writing*, we won't have to revisit the value of the Four Part Story Structure, because you already did that.

No? Okay, for an in-depth understanding, that book cuts to the meat of 4PSS. Go read that book. (Yep, shameless plug . . . again.)

Don't want to do that? It's okay, because we're going to use the 4PSS to write our beat sheet and scene outline later. For now, let's get clear on what story we're going to tell.

HIGH CONCEPT

The best way to understand concept is that it's the heart of your story—the essence of your tale. I know that borders on vague mushery, but here's what I mean:

The concept for your idea can best be described as a "what if?" question that begs for an answer from your reader. The best concepts cause anticipation of something exciting, new and different.

Describing high concept is as difficult as describing why you like a particular kind of music and not another, and why some people fall in love while others just shake their heads in confusion. Let's try to describe it anyway. Examples are always the best way, so. . .

EXAMPLES OF HIGH CONCEPT STORIES

A new idea

What if we told a story that was a parody of the lives of

the original Star Trek actors? (An idea) And what if, as they travel the washed-up-actor speaking circuit, they bump into some real aliens who ask them for help? Then, what if they're actually transported up into space and they have to live their own television series for real? And along their galactic way, they get into hilarious mayhem, while actually rising to their former pretended glory? - *Galaxy Quest*

A mash-up of two genres

I used the cowboys-and-aliens example in another book, but it's a great example of a non-traditional mash-up. What if cowboys from the Old West had to fight technologically advanced aliens in order to save the future of mankind? Expanding it—what if the cowboy who had the technology to defeat the aliens, turned out to be an outlaw but had amnesia from being abducted, so now he wanted to turn good? *Cowboys and Aliens*—a great concept. (Don't even get me started on *Firefly*.)

A concept is not only an idea, it's an intriguing question that spurs the imagination of the reader.

A new twist on an age-old genre

Cabin in the Woods is one of my all-time favorite horror movies. It's got everything—slashers, killer zombies, a scary "Evil Dead" vibe cabin and a bunch of horny dumb twentysomethings that make you wonder why you care if they get killed or not. But there's something else, too. Something underneath all of the gratuitous sex and bloodletting. Beneath the cabin in the woods is a secret, and when it's revealed it's almost a genre killer. Meaning, how would you top this?

Or how about love across the centuries?

This is right off of the Internet Movie Database: A lonely doctor who once occupied an unusual lakeside home begins exchanging love letters with its former resident, a frustrated architect. They must try to unravel the mystery behind their extraordinary romance before it's too late. - *The Lake House*

What if a pair of would-be lovers were separated in time and carried on a love affair through the mail separated by time?

Ask yourself what if, and then let your mind run wild with possibilities. They really are endless.

That last example gives me an idea. Remember before when we talked about stealing like an artist? Well, blockbuster movie summaries are a great place to explore ideas and concepts for your story.

:: ACTION ITEM

Go look at some popular movie summaries on IMDB. Summaries in the genre you want to write about. Take a few of the more popular ones and see if you can use bits and pieces from each one to come up with an entirely new and cool idea. In fact, let's do it right now!

Our own little story example

For *Dixxon—Teen Witch*, I searched the 10 best witch movies ever made and added a few ideas of my own. And since what Lise and I have talked about is a series that's a mash-up of different paranormal creature genres, werewolves, vampires, fairies, trolls and shapeshifters may appear as well. And since this is going to be a YA (young adult) series, we're going to need some teen angst in there in the form of a boyfriend who's a bit "unusual" himself.

IMDB Examples

Practical Magic—Sally and Gillian Owens use practical magic. But their magic comes with a curse: the men they fall in love with are doomed to an untimely death.

The Craft—A newcomer to a Catholic prep high school

falls in with a trio of outcast teenage girls who practice witchcraft. They all conjure up various spells and curses against those who even slightly anger them.

Beautiful Creatures—Ethan longs to escape his small Southern town. He meets a mysterious new girl, Lena. Together, they uncover dark secrets about their respective families, their history and their town. As they fall in hopeless love, of course.

Underworld—Selene, a beautiful vampire warrior, entrenched in a war between the vampire and werewolf races. Although she's aligned with the vampires, she falls in love with Michael, a human who's sought by werewolves for unknown reasons.

Van Helsing—The notorious monster hunter is sent to Transylvania to stop Count Dracula who is using Dr. Frankenstein's research and a werewolf for some sinister purpose.

Thanks to Internet Movie Database (IMDB) online for all of those summaries.

Our own little story's "what if?" question

Dixxon: Teen Witch—What if the last white witch, the only supernatural being who could bring balance to the worlds of magic and mortals, was a 15-year-old girl named Dixxon? A girl who had no idea that she was about to become the most powerful witch who would ever again be born.

And what if, on Dixxon's sixteenth birthday, that power revealed itself in the most insane and unexpected way? And what if in doing so, she finally caught the eye of the boy she liked for what seemed like forever? A boy who just happened to be a supernatural creature himself? Now, the very evil that threatens to destroy mankind is after Dixxon's new boyfriend, too.

7
THEMES

THEMES

Reading between the lines

The theme of your story is the unwritten philosophical position that your story takes. Never directly stated nor clubbed over your reader's head, theme is the chocolate fudge dripped delicately over the ice cream of your novel. The tale is tasty without it, but a powerful theme is just the little something extra that makes it exquisite.

All that metaphorical mushery aside, just what the hell is theme, anyway? In short, theme is what your story is about—the point of it.

Top 10 Hollywood movie themes:

1. Good vs. evil (Yes, but which is which?)
2. Love conquers all (Isn't that wonderful. . .)
3. Triumph over adversity (rags to riches!)
4. Man (woman) vs. society (rage against the machine!)

5. Battle—literal or metaphorical (Hollywood loves killing!)
6. Death as a part of life (not my favorite)
7. Revenge (my personal favorite)
8. Lost innocence (Haven't we all been here?)
9. Man (woman) vs. self (Inner demons anyone?)
10. Man (woman) vs. nature (Armageddon, yes!)

These are overdone, overused, and overly enjoyable to readers, because most of us are looking for entertainment and distraction, maybe a little meaning and perspective on top like a cherry. However, there are other themes that are nuances or drill-downs to those common ones:

- Power corrupts
- Sacrifice of self for others
- Unbridled power oppresses and destroys
- Love is war
- Beauty is subjective
- Good is gray
- Evil is not always bad
- Every system is corrupt
- Participating in a system gives it legitimacy
- Sometimes love conquers all . . . for the worse
- Revenge truly is sweet
- Love in the unlikeliest of places

Examples of themes

You may think that the **Hunger Games** is about Katniss Everdeen. It's actually about government authoritarian rule and oppression as seen through the eyes of one of its victims.

Cloud Atlas, which is just an insanely complicated and theme-packed book/movie that will take more than one read or viewing to understand all of it, is packed with the themes of "soul is forever and what you do today echoes into your eternity."

Is **Star Wars** about Luke Skywalker and Darth Vader? Nope. Classic good vs. evil. But that leads me to another point.

Secondary themes

In *Star Wars*, one secondary theme is man (Luke Skywalker) vs. himself. Luke must learn to overcome his fear in order to face Darth Vader and save the world from evil.

Themes are the things that make us think as we read or watch them unfold and play out. We identify with common themes, because everyone experiences them in some way or another.

Your theme is where you get to rage against your own machine—speak to your own beliefs and prejudices. But be careful, it's a fine line between raging between the lines and ranting to your reader. No one likes a rant, true though it may be.

Trust me, my hypocrite meter just pegged as I wrote that last paragraph of advice. (I'm a bit heavy-handed with my opinions in my novels. Which is to say nothing of these non-fiction books, as you're well aware of by now.)

WISK
"You're you and there is no other."

Finding your "voice"

Human beings are different by design. Each one of us experiences and sees and understands the exact same things . . . differently. Call it perspective or call it prejudice, no two writers write alike. And no two readers will read your story the same way or get the same message out of it. What will remain consistent is your writer "voice."

When I sprinkle "Darth Vader" throughout my non-fiction series and pepper my novels with sarcastic cynicism and wit, via statements from my characters like, "Leave it to me to arrive in Hell on the day the Devil gets

Alzheimer's" . . . that's my writer "voice." Only it's really my voice as tempered and toe-tipped into my stories just enough that I'm not writing opinion pieces disguised as novels.

Only that's exactly what many of us do in telling our stories. Even that's okay as long as the story is compelling and not just an autobiography that you think is interesting, but no one else does. However, art is as subjective as love, so it's a fine line. But here's an example of someone who successfully blended the line.

One of my heroes, Andrew Vachss

Authors write for a million reasons. One of the biggest ones is to reach people, deliver a message. Andrew Vachss—one of my favorite grizzled veteran authors (the guy's got an eye patch. How freakin' cool is that!)—used to be a child advocate lawyer. He found that he reached more people with the message of his cause by writing fiction about child endangerment issues than he ever did defending children in court. He took his very real and very concerned voice and put it into his fiction. His fire for it burns into his writing and people love it and learn about the depths of a societal problem that they may have never known existed otherwise.

Bury your opinion in your theme.

You have a reason that you write. You're passionate about that reason and your voice is the way you express that passion. Voice is style, panache, the way you dress, the way you speak and the way you view the world. You need to learn to speak in that voice, because it's authentic and real. The best way to do that is to stop censoring yourself when you start writing fiction.

Watch out for your inner critic.

We all go through life trying to say the right things in the right situations to the right people at the right times. It's how we avoid inviting open public ridicule—a defense mechanism we learned to stay out of the line of fire.

But fiction is about getting out of your comfort zone and into the unknown scary dark forest of your mind. Run into the woods screaming, instead of hiding behind a tree, hoping you don't get eaten by some imaginary beast.

You have things you want to say. If you can't say them out loud, do what a lot of authors do—write them down. I'm not saying blast your opinion all over your pages like blood splatter. I'm saying that if you're annoyed at something, let your character show that annoyance . . . out in the open.

One of the best ways to do this is to build your voice into your theme. If you hate authority, write anti-authoritarian tales. If you love gooey romance, write about your wildest romantic fantasies and be authentic about them.

:: ACTION ITEM

The next time you're talking to a trusted friend, take notice of the way you speak. How you talk when you don't fear consequences is your writer voice. Once you find that, your stories will take on a tone of truthfulness that can't be faked.

THE PREP WORK'S IMPORTANT

Finding ideas, turning those ideas into concepts, understanding the hero's journey, building in themes and finding your own voice are all part of the prep work that you have to do before you ever outline your novel. In reality, they're as much a part of outlining as sketching out a list of scenes.

There are more things—character development, villains, vocabulary selection, scene and setting building—that would be better covered outside this book. That doesn't mean I don't think they're important, that just means that the scope of this book won't be able to do them justice.

That being said, let's swing the lightsaber at 'em anyway. Hah! I had you there, didn't I?

8
SETTINGS AND VOCABULARY

SETTINGS

Where does your story take place?

Chances are your novel will take place—your first one, at least—in a limited number of physical locations. This keeps things manageable and allows you to focus on your story rather than world-building and describing each time your scene location changes. Three or four main places that require description in enough detail to give the reader a feeling of "place" should be sufficient.

Does your setting support your theme?

Settings should, but don't have to, go along with the theme of your story. Authoritarian rule is best played out against the bleak backdrop of decaying urban sprawl or tattered and run-down villages that exist in poverty next to the opulence and gluttony of the ruling class.

The best settings are characters themselves. Worlds in transition. A dying planet that our hero must escape from could underscore and parallel him or her running from the law for being unjustly accused of something.

Example:

I opened *The Fallen* series with a man running for his life from the authorities and set it all against the cold rainy backdrop of Seattle for two reasons. One, the constant gray underscored my theme of the line between good and evil being one of perspective. The other was that I lived there and knew and felt the setting for myself—it was easy to imagine and write it.

In movies, a viewer gets to visually experience the setting and it'll make them feel the way the theme of the movie wants them to. In your novel, you'll have to describe your setting to your reader to support the feeling you want to convey.

A description example

"The fog pressed down on the tops of the skyscrapers, like a huge sponge that just wouldn't dry out."

That line gives my reader a clear understanding that the world they're entering is oppressively damp. And the "pressing" verbiage parallels the authoritarian rule of the time and place.

Some story setting examples

You ever notice that Hollywood rarely buries someone on screen unless it's pouring down rain? There have to be umbrellas and wet, and black and gray tones and crying. It's complete cliche, but that's the setting supporting the scene.

Think about how you'd feel about a funeral where someone was being buried at a cemetery next to a warm and wonderful sandy beach. In fact, when Hollywood wants to inject some comic relief or irony into a scene, they often set it in an environment exactly opposite from where the scene would logically take place.

In *The Big Lebowski*, John Goodman and Jeff Bridges go to the ocean to spread their dead friend's ashes—return him to the sea. As Goodman tries to pour the ashes out of the urn, the wind whips up and covers him and Bridges in their friend's remains. That scene wouldn't work or be as rudely funny at a cemetery in the rain.

Our own little story

We needed a town. Lise and I decided on Louisiana as the place for us to set a story about witches and creatures and magic and witch burning. The folklore around the bayou state is rich and superstition still survives there. So I started the research.

Coming up with a short list of real towns in Louisiana proved pretty easy: Covington, coven of witches; Kilbourne, a bit too literal for part of our story; Sulphur, which we liked because it had a synonym that was perfect—brimstone, as in "fire and brimstone." We adapted Sulphur to suit us a little better and the "puritan punk" town of Brimstone Hill was born.

The Puritan Punk part is the fallen-apart humanity of Brimstone Hill, 100 years in the future.

:: ACTION ITEM

Here's one of the first steps I take in creating a fictitious world for a novel: **Create a master spreadsheet.** In that spreadsheet I have several tabs or sheets: a special vocabulary sheet, a settings sheet—one for each physical location—and a character sheet for each logical grouping of people.

For instance, in *Dixxon* there are three basic types of characters for the first book—witches (including their animals), wolves, and townspeople. Each of these groups has unique naming characteristics and speech patterns. I put information like character descriptions, patterns of speech, quirks and mannerisms, what their name "means," and their backstory in rows in my spreadsheet.

That way, when I lose track—which does happen—I can refer to my master spreadsheet.

For settings, to understand the unique locations and surroundings I'm working with, I ask myself questions like:

- Where are we?
- What time period are we in?
- Are we in the future, the past, the present?
- Where does my hero live?
- What are the different locations that'll appear in this novel?
- What does the surrounding area look like?
- Are there particular landmarks my reader should know about?
- What do most people do in "heroville?"
- What are the people who live there like?
- Do the residents like "heroville" or hate having to live there?
- What creatures and animals and things "grow" or lurk there?
- What's the weather like?
- Is my world dark, light, magic, mortal, miserable, happy, sad, wonderful. . .?
- What evil lurks in your world?

- Does my hero live in a mansion, a hut or a cardboard box?
- Is this a fantastic world, another planet, or simply a fictional portrayal of the "real" world?

Answer these questions and add it to the description of each location in your master spreadsheet to keep track of your world.

VOCABULARY LIST

In your world, you'll no doubt have slang and invented words and a list of vocabulary that's peculiar or particular to your world. If you don't, you probably should.

Every world, culture, system and planet has its own slang and way of speaking.

In our own little story

In Dixxon's world, a combination of voodoo Creole and Elizabethan proper English will have emerged, as societal meltdown caused a melding of the voodoo superstitions within Louisiana southern high society.

As I told you, I keep my lists for vocabulary in my master spreadsheet document and refer to it often. It's especially helpful when I'm writing dialogue, littered with phrases and common colloquialisms for the time and world. Not only that, but you'll find yourself making a common habitual error as you write fast—your characters will all start to sound alike. It helps to pause and revisit your spreadsheet to get clear on the nuanced differences between all of your characters.

QUICK TIP:

The best thing about having vocabulary in a master spreadsheet—Excel, Google Docs spreadsheet or spreadsheet of your choice—instead of inside Scrivener or a Word document is that as you add terms and it becomes difficult to keep track of them, you can sort the columns alphabetically to make searching easier.

9
RESEARCH

RESEARCH

Whatever you may think fiction writing is, there's a lot of research. Maybe almost as much as non-fiction, but I feel like it's a lot more fun, because you get to let your imagination run wild.

I like to weave truth into fiction.

In researching people and places you'll find all sorts of cool things to fit into your story.

For instance, in the 1940s in our inspiration town, Sulphur, they dug a channel to the ocean to transport oil by barge. And we had our body of water—a lake that spilled over the edges of that river in hurricane season—where frogs "ribbit" out warnings and send messages up and down the riverbank that witches can understand because they can speak to animals.

And the first Catholic church was built on some land dubbed the "richest 50 acres in the world," because it had sulphur under it. Also, spirits in voodoo are known as Loa; they're represented by Catholic saint lithographs.

During slavery in Haiti, white French masters prohibited slaves from pursuing voodoo as a religion and anyone caught practicing any religion other than Catholicism was severely punished. The slaves, still deeply attached to their African roots, used Catholic saint images during voodoo ceremonies, pretending to be praying to them while in their heart they were praying to their African gods.

So instead of Catholicism emerging in our new world, there's a hybrid voodoo-Catholicism religion that prays to dark spirits and burns magic folk at the stake, especially witches, to appease God.

Just keep filling in the blanks.

We needed a town, a dark forest, a river/lake, a schoolhouse/church, a broken-down castle for Dixxon to live in, and a far-off dark location for our wicked witch council to convene. So Brimstone Hill, the Frasch Forest (named for one of the town of Sulphur's original founders), Prien Lake (a real lake near our town), the Kalkashoo River (the phonetic spelling of its actual name, by the way), and the dark magic lake to the southwest of our real research town—Black Lake (another real location).

And in the middle of Black Lake, a place where the witch council convenes to decide the fate and future of magic, is Bile Island—the nastiest, most dangerous place any non-magic being can find themselves.

QUICK TIP:

One of the best ways to get inspiration for your novel is by researching it. Pay particular attention as you look up things like locations, names, customs and regional information. Some of the best fiction ideas come from the underlying truth in your research.

10
CHARACTERS

THE MONOMYTH

WISK

"Mono—what? Isn't that some kind of disease?"

Far from it. On second thought, heroism could potentially be a disease. We authors have a strong case of it, that's for sure. But this is the next critical piece of your novel's puzzle. Before you begin, you must have a hero that your audience can root for or at minimum hate that they love him or her. Once we do that, we send our hero on a dangerous quest.

Novels are about the hero's journey.

The monomyth is a pattern of storytelling found in many cultures scattered throughout the world and separated by time such that common themes in their storytelling styles emerged. It's a 17-stage narrative pattern of the hero's journey of self-discovery. A pattern that just so happens to overlay on top of the Four Part Story Structure rather well. Or maybe it's the other way around?

Time for Jedi training?

"I pull out my lightsaber and fire up the red light. I want them to pay attention to this next part. Funny thing about a glowing red beam of light that can cut your arm off—no one ignores you when you're swinging it around."

Simplifying the basic storytelling structure

Darth Vader threats aside, after studying story structure six ways from Tuesday, I think I can boil this information down into some nice easy lightsaber-severed-sized chunks for you. Here they are:

There's an old Roman saying—"Veni, vidi, vici." I came, I saw, I conquered. It's a Latin phrase used by Julius Caesar to refer to a swift, conclusive victory. Which, by the way, is horrible storytelling.

Conflict and struggle and near-death defeat, followed by eventual and costly triumph is the literal or metaphorical stuff of great stories. So I would rewrite Caesar this way, because he left one part of his fantastic story out.

4PSS overlaid onto that statement: I came, I saw, *I was nearly killed*, and then I conquered.

Transformation is storytelling.

The monomyth is about transformation—the stuff of great novels. Challenges that are put to an unwilling or unwitting hero to force them to participate in their own story and evolve because of it. Then, eventually, though the odds are stacked heavily against them, our heroes fight and win the day, win the guy/girl, and ride into the sunset, forever changed.

The best heroes are flawed, ordinary people thrust into extraordinary circumstances beyond their control. They somehow rise to the occasion and will never again be the way they were before. Our characters are better people once we're done with them, but their transformation comes at the loss of something dear to them, even if it be their comfy delusions.

:: ACTION ITEM

Especially if you like westerns, the family movie, *Rango*, weaves in the hero's journey and nearly clubs you over the head with story structure so eloquently that I can think of no other story as directly sprinkled with the hero's journey. If you have kids, have an extra two hours lying around, or just want to see a high-concept story, watch it.

BONUS:

Watch for the scene at the beginning where Johnny Depp as Rango gives an ode to *Fear and Loathing in Las Vegas* (his movie), splatting on the car windshield of the characters from that story.

HEROES

Heroes are seemingly frail, oftentimes stupid at the outset of their stories, and many times so simplistically naive that it's a little difficult to get on their team when we first meet them. So try not to make them too idealistic, or too right, or too anything that's just not realistically damaged just a little bit by life.

Most of us don't make it out of high school without a demon or two growling along behind us. Even the star quarterback will come face to face with the fact that the NFL's not breaking down his door anytime soon. So give your hero some inner demons that will haunt him or her throughout your story. And it's great if you can tie those demons to something or someone that embodies those very things.

Female heroes rock.

Women want to be them and men love to watch them. And no discussion of female heroes should dare start without Ellen Ripley, played by Sigourney Weaver in *Aliens*. Not *Alien*—movie one—though that was a good story. But Ellen Ripley in *Aliens*, protecting her little Newt in the cargo bay of their spaceship from the evil alien queen? Get . . . outta here! Now there's one practical, powerful, and pissed-off hero for you.

By the time Ripley works her way into her own story and turns to fight in Part 3, she's had enough of evil businessmen sacrificing their own kind for profit; enough of incompetent and arrogant jarhead space marines; and enough of vicious, murdering, dripping-fanged alien "bitches!"

:: **ACTION ITEM**

Use your master spreadsheet and describe your characters. Start with your hero and answer these questions:

- What's your character's name?
- What does that name mean?
- How did they get that name?
- Where do they live?
- Who are their friends?
- How old are they?
- What do they secretly fear?
- What do they love?
- What do they wish for at night?
- What crazy food do they love?

- What words do they mispronounce?
- What annoying little habit do they have?
- What kind of clothes does your hero wear?
- What would they never wear?
- Who are your hero's friends?
- Does your hero have enemies?
- Who does your hero secretly wish they were with?

And the most important question of all:

What does your character want most desperately above anything and everything else? This one question gets its own column because that is the overarching motivation that drives every decision your hero makes.

QUICK TIP:

Create a character avatar.

Go on the Internet and find an image on a stock photography site that you think embodies your hero. Keep that handy as you write. Scrivener has a location for images and that's where I keep pictures that represent each one of my characters. (Import images into Scrivener.) If I get stuck when I'm writing, I take a quick peek at my character's avatar and it usually gives me an idea to get going again.

Even better, imagine you're making a movie of your novel and cast actors for all of your character parts. Then get images of those actor-characters and pull them inside Scrivener to refer to.

Example:

Lise thought that Amanda Seyfried from the movie *Red Riding Hood* would be very close to how our hero, Dixxon, would look and act in her own story. So we're using an image of her in that movie as an avatar for our Dixxon hero.

We simply imported that image into our Scrivener binder and put it in a "Characters" folder below our novel content. This has the added benefit that since we're co-authoring, we'll both have a similar and clear vision of what our hero looks and acts like.

Do the same for each of your characters.

VILLAINS

Your hero . . . needs a villain. For many reasons, but mainly as the impetus for them to grow beyond what they are now. Break your hero out of their delusions and force them to confront the thing they're most afraid of.

The best villains are ones that you hate that you love . . . just a little bit. They're deliciously devious and have genuinely redeeming qualities beneath all that bad. They make a certain ironic sense when they speak and truly believe that they're not so much evil as "unconventional" and misunderstood. Oh, and they just *know* that they're smarter than the average person, including your hero.

There's a particular righteousness in villains and what they want. Maybe it's revenge for a past injustice to them, maybe it's that there were circumstances beyond their control that morphed them into being mean, but rarely is it that they were born sociopaths.

Conflict is storytelling.

Storytelling is good vs. evil—conflict. Without that, stories aren't all that great. Villains give a hero something to fight against and someone for the reader to hate. They *are* conflict. But what happens when the villain is more fun than the hero?

Examples of great villains you can't help loving

Hannibal Lecter in *Silence of the Lambs*. We just love that he kills the annoyingly uncouth. And he helps FBI agent Clarice Starling track down a worse serial killer while at the same time helping her survive the FBI's misogynistic culture.

Tyler Durden in *Fight Club*. An anarchist after my own heart, the dark side of Edward Norton's mind, Tyler represents a hidden animalistic side just underneath the surface of civility in men. And when he speaks about society and its ills, we can't help but agree with him.

Heath Ledger's Joker in *The Dark Knight*. I mentioned this before, but he's just too delicious not to mention again. I'll admit to being a bit of an anti-authoritarian anarchist, and so yes I do cheer for bad guys to kill self-righteous good guys, but Heath was simply heavenly in this story.

No amount of "good" rationalization can make you fully disagree with what he's saying and why he's doing what he's doing. And he makes no differentiation between killing good guys and dispatching his own bad guys, which just further adds to the gray quality of the line between good and a bad that's just so bad it comes full circle back to good. Huh?

But, Darth, all those examples are men! What about the women?

I'm getting there.

Annie Wilkes in *Misery*. Okay, it's hard to like a villainess who imprisons an author and hobbles his feet with a sledgehammer, but think about that for a minute. Picture all the self-righteous, pompous, exclusionist M.A. graduates you've ever met, frowning on and disrespecting your dream to write. Wouldn't it be nice to "Kathy Bates" their feet?

Darth, you've completely lost it!

In a book, I meant. In a fiction novel. I would never do that for real.

And finally, what brief glimpse into female villainy would be complete without Sharon Stone? And it's not just for her revealing interrogation scene in *Basic Instinct*, either.

Catherine Tramell in *Basic Instinct* is so deliciously manipulating, so wonderfully believable and so seductively forgivable, that most of us men know we'd have been caught in her web of lies . . . easily.

CHARACTERS

A hero, a villain, a sidekick and a love interest—gotta have 'em. Okay, you don't have to do anything, but it's much more fun for your reader if you do.

Your story simply won't work without someone who the audience can root for or at least fear for a little. If no one cares about your hero, then no one cares about your story. Not good.

The best heroes are flawed characters that are just overly real enough that many people can identify with them. They may act worse or better, or be more completely open than anyone would be in "reality," but in fiction we love that about people.

In novels, characters love and curse and cry, and laugh at stupid jokes and pretend they like people when they don't or they just come right out and say it to their faces, daring them to do anything about it. Whoa! I got Darthed there a little bit.

A quickie about quirks

Characters talk funny and have quirks. Like one of my favorites: In the TV series *Burn Notice*, Michael, the hero hitman ex-CIA hunk guy, eats yogurt like he's grubbing popcorn at a movie. There are so many scenes with him spooning yogurt into his mouth as he and his sidekick and love interest plot their next spy game, that I find myself worrying for him in case he's lactose intolerant. I fret that he'll have to stop a mission in mid-battle to hit the bathroom or risk having an . . . accident.

Love interests

Let's stick with *Burn Notice*. Michael's "girlfriend," Fiona, is actually a freelance hitwoman herself. A waif of a love interest who in real life wouldn't have the muscle to lift the fork that she desperately needs to feed her face with, but in fiction can wield a 20-pound long-range sniper rifle with the strength and cold cunning of a she-wolf that just had a pup stolen from her den.

Her scrawny, less body fat than Linda Hamilton in *Terminator* arms aside, Fiona's job is to give Michael, the hero, hope for happiness in a "normal" life with her, not being pursued by the CIA. She grounds him in the reality of what they are—ex-trained killers who may or may not ever find love. She gives him hope, but she's also his haunting past.

Sidekicks

Sidekicks are funny characters. Sometimes you love them, sometimes they annoy the hell out of you and sometimes they're simply, beautifully more worldly-wise than our hero. Usually when they have to save our hero from his or her own delusions of right and wrong and good and evil and what has to be done versus what should be done.

If there's a dirty job to be done that will sully our hero in some way in our reader's eyes, we send the sidekick to "take one for the team."

Have to pose as a lady to infiltrate an enemy stronghold? Sidekick.

Need to dig a grave to bury the bodies you just assassinated? That's okay, hero, you go ahead with the ladies to the bar, I'll bury these bodies in the rain and mud and muck. No problem, no problem at all. Our dutiful sidekick.

Yes, girl sidekicks do the dirty, "nasty" jobs too.

Does the hunk that the hero would like to take up to her hotel room have a less-than-desirable wingman with an eye patch and a wooden leg and a disgusting sense of humor? Guess who sidekick-girl is limping up to their room with.

Michael's sidekick in *Burn Notice* is none other than *Evil Dead* cult icon Bruce Campbell. And he does such a fantastic job of playing his part as an ex-CIA "old-dog" that he often steals the scene and show from Michael. Sidekicks are like that.

Villains

I love villains. Mainly because I hate self-righteous ideologues who blindly believe in the lie that the world tells them. Was that my inner voice? Sorry. . .

Anyway, the best villains are ones that you hate that you love in some little way. They have a tragic story that has turned them evil, but they also have a point in their evil treachery. Even the evil ex-wife in a love story had a cheating father who left her mother and her to live in poverty. She may not boil a bunny on your porch, but she's keying our hero's car for a very good reason . . . in her mind, anyway.

Delicious villains

There's no better evil villain who makes a good point than Heath Ledger's portrayal of the Joker in *The Dark Knight*. As I watched him monologue. . . (I've said it before—all villains monologue. I would too if I had that much cool stuff to say.) Regardless, you can't help agreeing with the best of villainous characters.

Rarely does pure evil exist beside pure good. Everything in the world is shades of gray and I don't mean that "fun" kind in E.L. James' books. And that brings me to this. . .

Our own little story

Teen witch Dixxon's our hero, but who's our villain? Since we're writing a series, there'll be plenty of places to find them.

Is it the evil priest who teaches school in town? The Witch Council who wants to eliminate all of mankind? The "helpful" auntie assassin witch, sent to "take care of" Dixxon? Or is it the leader of the pack of werewolves in the woods? Maybe . . . it's the rich town girls that tease and taunt Dixxon at school? Or maybe . . . just maybe . . . it's all of them.

Whoever it is, do they know they're messing with the last white witch? I think not!

Dixxon's sidekick

Lise and I had a tough time brainstorming this, because we had to have someone to help our hero at first, but also someone to help her grow up. For that reason she got several sidekicks in the form of cats and brooms and a friend at school. (Dixxon's kind of a witchy Cinderella.) Unfortunately, in order for Dixxon to grow up—have her delusions and world turned upside down—one of them had to die. Ouch!

Love interests

Teen angst is usually about relationships and dating and high school. Think about it: *Hunger Games*—boyfriend . . . two of them! One hunky and strong and the other a cake decorator begging to be saved. Through the entire series Katniss has to ping-pong back and forth between them and which one she loves . . . more. Poor Katniss. . .

Divergent—boyfriend. *The Craft*—lovesick, crazed "boyfriend." Boyfriends of girl heroes, they're everywhere. Typically, in real life, they're someone about 5-10 years too old for the hero (from a dad of daughters perspective).

So, our Dixxon needed a boyfriend. Trouble was, he's not supposed to be around her. In fact, if her future love's pack leader—yep, he's a werewolf—has anything to say about it, Dixxon's future new boyfriend will be downright hazardous to her health.

The supporting characters

No matter how you slice it, there will be more characters the further you delve into your own story. After all, two people running around in circles with each other doesn't make for suspenseful or played-out drama (Tom Hanks on an island talking to a volleyball in *Castaway* aside). Of course, there are exceptions, but most stories will need a cast of characters to support the hero, help them grow, challenge them and confound them.

Dixxon's "cast" of characters

Love Interest—Bane, the future boyfriend.

Guardian—Magnolia, Dixxon's school "friend."

Antagonists—Aside from the Witch Council themselves, there's Auntie Maxxine the "friendly" witch sent to help. And Father Felixx LaFavroux, the witch-burning town priest.

Sidekicks—In Dixxon's own world, creatures abound. Frogs repeatedly "ribbit" warnings and messages that become the means for witches to communicate and send information, werewolves exist in the depths of the bayou and are called "croc dogs" by locals due to the French word for fang being "croc."

Not only are cats charged with protecting witches, but they speak to them in an upper-crust dialect more reminiscent of seventeenth century New Orleans than the future's guttural-voodoo superstitious townspeople.

Example:

"The forest?" Baxxter purred. "What a dreadful notion. And at this hour? Simply out of the question."

But one of the coolest "characters" will be the house that protects Dixxon from harm—her mansion.

Dixxon's den—the Mangy Mansion. It's a run-down, dusty, broken porch vile of voodoo and venomous hidden secrets. It coughs dust that broom-sweeps under its rugs, it expels intruders like the Addams Family's haunted house, and deep underneath its main staircase is a secret passageway to the dark and dangerous Frasch Forest (named after one of Brimstone Hill's (Sulphur, LA) real founders in our backstory research).

Remember, don't be afraid to weave the real in with the imagined.

SOME OTHER GREAT CHARACTER TYPES

While we're on the subject of characters, here's a list of some of the archetypical characters who can play along with our hero:

- **Mentor**—anyone who teaches and protects the hero
- **Guardian**—a menacing force that threatens

- the hero
- **Herald**—a force that brings a new challenge to the hero
- **Shapeshifter**—characters who change constantly
- **Shadow**—character who represents the dark side
- **Ally**—someone who travels with the hero on their journey
- **Trickster**—embodies mischief and desire for change

The lines between these blur and some of them can be wrapped together in one character. You don't have to use all of them, but knowing that they're there to call upon helps.

You can sprinkle some or all of these characters throughout your novel, but each usually has a function only in relation to the hero's own quest. They either help, hinder, challenge, confuse, betray or accompany our hero on his or her quest.

Incidental characters

Outside of those functions, all the others are incidental characters who help logically drive scenes.

Example:

If our hero and his love interest need to get across town to the Billionaire's Benefit Ball, they might need to take a taxi. Especially if they want to pass the time with a little hanky-panky on the way. What? It's just an idea—50 shades, remember?

Regardless, we don't have to give the taxi driver much to do outside of driving and occasionally peeking in his rearview mirror. We certainly don't need to give him or her a lengthy description and extra dialogue.

Give them a description like "The taxi driver's demeanor was as gruff as the hair on his face. He barely said anything the entire trip, but he watched. I knew he would watch. That's what I wanted."

Backstory

A character's backstory is everything that happened to them before the start of your novel. It's why they are who they are, why they do and say the things they do, and why they're real to our readers. Our characters' backstories define them.

Backstories guide our characters' actions. You have to know what they are, so you know how your characters will react to any given situation.

Think about your own life. Everything you are. The way you react to things and the way you speak, act and live are functions and shadows of every experience you've had in your entire life. Some experiences are more harrowing and embedded in our psyches than others, and that's what we focus on in our character's backstory—defining moments that made them who they are and act the way they do.

Example:

A serial killer who hunts down pedophiles and dismembers them (Remember our suitcase full of body parts news headline from before?) may have been abused as a child. And our hero—special victims unit detective—may be faced with the very real dilemma that he figured out who this "bad guy" is only to find out that the people the bad guy is killing are the very ones he's trying to stop.

And then our hero will face a dilemma: Is the serial killer just a faster means to the end he's after in the first place? Should he let the serial killer escape and keep cleaning up the "real" bad guys? A moral dilemma.

But maybe our hero has something buried in his own past that makes him let the serial killer go. Maybe he knew someone once whom he could have saved had he done the "wrong" thing. Will he right that mistake in his haunting backstory?

Our own little story

Dixxon doesn't know where she came from. As far as she knows, she's always lived in her mansion with Cat and Broom. But she has a past. Dixxon's parents broke a cardinal rule of magic—they mixed magic and mankind and had Dixxon. At least one of them was killed for it. Now, though Cat and Broom may know the truth of it, Dixxon doesn't know who or what she is.

Don't cheat your secondary characters' backstory.

Everyone gets backstory. It helps enrich your story. In ours, the evil auntie and the cruel minister of voodoo at the town church have "history" together. And one of them has a secret about the depths of the treachery in that history. We'll reveal it over the course of the series. But if evil auntie's backstory ever catches up to her. . . She'll wish she weren't a witch.

Dixxon's boyfriend has backstory too—or more importantly his pack leader has a history with witches. Now, the entire pack is prohibited from associating with witches, let alone getting "involved" with one.

Cat used to be a fairy godmother, and Broom. . .? Well, Broom has a dark secret that even he doesn't realize. The frogs almost went extinct because of human beings destroying the planet and they're none too happy about that. So they play tricks on human beings.

And the dwarves? Well, if being three feet tall weren't a bad enough aftereffect of the old world meltdown, now they're relegated to being spies for their taller human counterparts. And that game has them cooking up some potions of their own.

QUIRKS, HABITS AND MANNERISMS

Characters have favorite words, habits, ways of doing things. Things they like and things they hate.

In one of my early novels that I have yet to republish, my hero and her detective sidekick loved to go to J.D.'s Pancake House for breakfast before starting the day finding bad guys.

My tall slender police lieutenant lady who never gained an ounce of weight in her life no matter what she ate, loved French toast with butter and peanut butter on top, smothered in maple syrup. And it just happened to be the way that her hulky but slightly pudgy sidekick—a secret ex-naval intelligence detective—won his swooning way into her heart. He brought her breakfast in a bag in a scene in which, when my wife read it she had to stop and ask, "Why don't you do that for me?"

Obviously a pain point I'll have to work on. "But honey, this is fiction."

Our own little story

Dixxon loves to walk along the shores of Prien Lake at night, collecting roots and weeds and mushrooms for her special tea. She sings little magic spells as she goes, but she has no idea what they mean or what they do.

Cat spins three times to the left before scratching down into the couch to sleep. And Broom has a nasty habit of sweeping the last swish of dirt under the rug in the sitting room, causing the Mangy Mansion to cough dust out the back porch.

QUICK TIP:

A note on character descriptions.

Backstory, height, weight, build, eyes are obvious things to detail, but in describing your characters, you also want to let the reader inject themselves into the story. Give them a character outline and then let them fill in the blanks.

Example:

Jeb was a hard, long-muscled man, made that way from chopping wood every spring to stack in rigid rows along the back fence. Those rows stood all summer long, drying to tough tinder, never moving, never faltering, waiting for their moment to be turned into raw raging fire . . . just like Jeb.

There's a lot left out of that character description, but also a lot for the reader to fill in. And later in the story we'll make sure to fill in the blanks by using perspectives from other characters and situational descriptions of Jeb.

:: ACTION ITEM

Give everyone backstories, character descriptions, quirks and habits, and make everyone relatable. Make them just flawed enough to be human. Yes, even the supernatural, because the best fantasy, sci-fi or otherworldly stories are merely human struggles disguised as fantastic effects and supernatural events.

If you haven't yet, now's the time to create that master spreadsheet and start cataloging and tracking your characters' details.

11
STORY SUMMARIES

WISK

(Okay, I'm letting Inigo Montoya from *The Princess Bride* hijack it this time.)

Westley: "Who are you? Are we enemies? Why am I on this wall? Where is Buttercup?"
Inigo Montoya: "Let me explain."
[pause]
Inigo Montoya: "No, there is too much. Let me sum up: Buttercup is marrying Humperdinck in little less than half an hour. So all we have to do is get in, break up the wedding, steal the princess, make our escape ... after I kill Count Rugen."

SUMMARIES

In order to start our story we have to be able to state clearly and succinctly what it's about. A summary gives you and your reader a quick and easy way to determine if the story will be interesting to them or not.

Stories have a beginning, a middle and an ending. So

does your summary. We start small and then expand it, because you'll have several uses for a fiction summary.

Uses for your summary:

- Your book's description page on Amazon, Nook, Kobo, etc.
- The back jacket of the print version of your book.
- Submitting your book to marketing sites.
- Telling someone who asks you what your novel's about. (Believe me, the first time you look a friend in the eye and have no idea how to explain your story, you'll realize you need to go back and write a better summary.)

Three-word summary

Okay, it can be three to five to seven words, but this is a short bullet point that distills your story down to unmistakable simplicity. They're often written as movie taglines, distilling the story but also inviting a mystery to be solved.

Dixxon—Teen Witch is a title, but "The last white witch must save mankind" is a summary that alludes to, but doesn't spoil the story. It also asks a question: "Why is she the last one?"

Three-word summary examples:

Boy wizard wonder fights evil—*Harry Potter*
One woman battles space monsters bent on eating her—*Aliens*
Greed leads to one place—*Wall Street*
Love Lost in London—A fictitious romance set in Great Britain, maybe.

Or try distilling it to beginning, middle and end in as few words as possible. The following sound bite is often attributed to Hemingway, but accounts of it before him make that suspect. For our purposes, we don't care, but it still makes great author-cocktail party-filler conversation.

"For sale: baby shoes, never worn."

Another way to write your smallest summary is the three-phrase explanation:

"One nice nun. One not-so-nice priest. One big secret."

The idea is to distill your story down to a small bite-sized morsel that sounds like it would be tasty and at the very least makes sense. It's nice if it begs the reader to ask a question. It should intrigue someone to read the larger single-sentence-sized summary or paragraph summary on the book jacket or description page.

:: ACTION ITEM

Go write a quick three-to-nine-word blurb that distills your story and explains it without giving away the end. Take one of the themes and use it for a template. Write it five different ways until you can describe it to your own satisfaction and then run it by a friend.

One-sentence summary

It's hard to pack that much information into one sentence, but that's the stuff of novels—conveying as much by what you don't say as by what you do. The story between the lines of your story—unspoken but silently understood.

A good one-sentence summary has three elements:

1. Introduce your hero.
2. Set them on a quest.
3. Give them consequences.

One-sentence summary examples:

Cowboys and Aliens—Aliens attack a town in the Old West and the townspeople must find them before they destroy the future of Earth.

The Fifth Element—In the future, a cab driver unwittingly becomes the central figure in the search for a legendary cosmic weapon to keep evil from taking over the universe.

Our own little story's one-sentence summary

Dixxon—By the next full moon, the last white witch must bring balance to the futuristic realms of magic and mankind . . . or risk the ruin of both.

:: ACTION ITEM

Try it. Write a one-sentence summary that introduces your hero, gives them a quest, and states the consequences for failure.

One-paragraph summary

Now it's getting a little easier, but all that short and sweet in the previous two helps us. Because once we start expanding, we're already working with good raw material. Simply put a little more detail around your already very succinct explanation.

Our own little story's paragraph summary:

One hundred years in the future, magic exists alongside humanity in a delicate truce. But the balance that's survived for thousands of years has tipped to the point of breaking. Dixxon barely has time to wonder if she can handle a new boyfriend, let alone realize that she's actually the last white witch. Will she be able to save them, or will the realms plunge into darkness at the next full moon? Either way, love isn't a potion to be fooled with.

A paragraph makes it a little clearer that Dixxon is a magical person with a big responsibility, but also a girl who's about to experience some seriously complicated "magic" in the form of love.

DESCRIPTION

This expands on our one-paragraph summary. We want to go to the point of making the story intriguing, stopping short of giving away the entire plot. A mini 4PSS in here helps. Introduce your hero, warn of impending conflict to them, hint at the stakes for failure, and give them a ticking-clock time limit.

Our own little story's description example:

Dixxon has all the normal worries and wants of any average fifteen-year-old girl. But though she doesn't know it yet, she's also the last white witch. She's ordained to bring balance and peace back between the magical and the mortal worlds. That's a tall order for a girl who's entertaining ideas about her first boyfriend.

To make matters worse, Dixxon's "boyfriend" has a pretty hairy secret of his own. If she knew any better, Dixxon might keep him on a shorter leash. But the magic of love blinds all and neither of them can see what's coming next.

If Dixxon doesn't figure out and fulfill her destiny by the next full moon, she may never get that boyfriend, but it won't be the worst of magic and mankind's worries. Because love may conquer all in the mortal world, but it'll take a stronger potion than that to save magic from itself.

THE CRUX OF YOUR STORY

Getting your hero what he or she wants

You can get lost in all the details of creating worlds and characters and the fun of descriptions and scenes, but you have to remain focused on the job of your outline— driving your hero through his or her quest to a satisfying climax/conclusion.

To that end, we need to describe what our hero wants and has to get on his or her quest. That will help us stay on track.

Maybe your hero wants to win the affections of a man or

girl or boy, as the case may be. Maybe they want to be rich, having come from poverty. Or maybe they just want to escape prison badly enough that they're willing to do anything to get out.

Whatever it is, that underlying want will drive your hero through his or her story. It *is* your story.

Crux example:

In *Harry Potter,* throughout the entire series, Harry's deepest desire was to have known his parents. That drives him through his story. And you see that at any and every opportunity, Harry will sidetrack himself or get into trouble over being tempted with some knowledge of his parents.

Our own little story's crux example:

Dixxon always assumed that her parents were witches. And as far as she's concerned, they both died long before she could remember anything about them. At least that's what Cat and Broom have told her. The truth? Well, the truth is wrapped in a lie that just walked through the front door of the Mangy Mansion. Now, Dixxon's need to know the real story about her mother and father is blinding her to "Auntie's" tempting tales of the past.

The reality is that Dixxon's parents weren't both witches. Her mother was a mortal and the Witch Council condemned her to death for it, but not before she secretly had Dixxon. The worst part—her own father was the witch who was supposed to carry out the sentence.

:: ACTION ITEM

Figure out what your hero wants. A desperate desire that they need fulfilled more than anything in the world. Write it down as if you were listening to one of your closest friends tell you a secret. As always, add it to your master spreadsheet.

12
BEAT SHEET OUTLINE

WISK

"I'm just plum backed up with backstory. Let's plot this thing!"

Not . . . just . . . yet.

FIRST, LET'S TALK ABOUT BEATS

A beat is the smallest unit of storytelling. It's a piece of the story where a single event happens. Outlining can be simply stated as stringing these beats together. In movie scripting, that process is called creating a beat sheet.

A beat sheet is an entire story told beat by beat—step by step. It keeps the primary story (your hero's journey) and the secondary story line (maybe the underlying love interest story) and any other minor story lines (your villain's backstory, for instance) separated. A beat sheet helps you weave those together in the order you want them to happen. It helps with logical flow.

A beat sheet is as long or short as it needs to be to tell the story efficiently. Because we don't want any single act to get weighted too heavily with one story line. The hero's story usually has more beats than the underlying love story, and they both get more than the villain's backstory.

How many beats there are depends on the pace of the storytelling. A dialogue-heavy story will get fewer beats per section than an action story.

The point of writing a beat sheet first is to allow you to get a clear sense of the way the story will flow. The beats should be clear and simple and tell you where you are physically in your story. This helps with understanding where your scene breaks should be.

In your beat sheet, explain what happens in each beat and move on. Tell your story in broad strokes.

SCENES

Scenes are individual and unique locations within a beat section.

The Four Part Story Structure consists of, amazingly enough, four parts. Within each of those parts are beats. The inciting incident, for example, is a beat. Each beat may have several scenes—locations—in it.

There's a technique in screenwriting that's used to outline a script. It works pretty well for fiction novel scene outlining. Simply put, at the beginning of each scene, you state the location of the scene. If your location changes, that's a new scene.

And even as I'm reading this, I can tell that it would be better explained as an example.

Example:

Part 1 of a bank robbery story may start off at the Opening Scene beat like this:

The Beat - Criminals rob a bank.

1. Scene 1 - Ext. (Exterior) Bank - Day - Robbers talk in the getaway car just outside the bank.
2. Scene 2 - Ext. Bank - Day - Robbers get out of the car and go into the bank.
3. Scene 3 - Int. (Interior) Bank - Day - Robbers shoot up the bank and get the money.
4. Scene 4 - Ext. Bank - Day - Robbers run out and drive off.

And that's the end of the "Criminals rob a bank" opening beat.

STRUCTURE IS STORY

Understanding story structure, beats and scenes allows you to break your story down into bite-sized chunks that make sense, logically flow and get everyone in your story from point A to point Z.

The essence of outlining is that roadmap we talked about at the beginning of this book. A beat sheet boils that down into specific weigh points along the road to your destination.

QUICK TIP:

Treat each scene and each beat as the only thing you have to worry about next. This helps compartmentalize the daunting task of writing a large novel.

By outlining your novel beforehand, you can also choose to skip to a section that you have a brilliant idea about and write that scene or beat out as the inspiration strikes you.

Our own little story's beat sheet:

Here's our beat sheet for Dixxon. We're careful to make it a working document and not flesh out too many of the details as we go. We want a skeleton that we can use to fill in the blanks of our story later in our Four Part Story Structure detailed working summary.

BEAT BY BEAT

Part 1 - Setup

Beat 1 - Opening Scene and Hook

Scene - Ext. Frasch Forest - Night
A woman is about to be burned at the stake in the woods. A woman witch prevents a man witch from saving her. Then she banishes the man witch from the kingdom of witches, the Black Lake.

Scene - Ext. Mangy Mansion - Night
Our teen witch hero, Dixxon, wakes up from this dream. It's the middle of the night and she's yelling for her friends, Cat and Broom. They tell her she's had another nightmare. The dreams are getting worse as it approaches Dixxon's sixteenth birthday—the next full moon. A blue moon.

She tells Cat that she needs to go for a walk in the moonlight to calm her nerves. Cat tries to warn her that the dark creatures are becoming more restless as the full moon approaches. Dixxon is out the door before he can stop her.

Scene - Ext. Along Prien Lake - Night
Dixxon likes to roam the shores of the lake. The edges of the lake teem with frogs and Dixxon sings little rhymes to them, reminiscent of spells. A howling wolf—music to Dixxon's ears normally—sounds stranger this night.

Scene - Ext. Frasch Forest - Night
Dixxon enters the dark forest, headed to her favorite clearing to watch the moon. The howling turns to screeching and then scuffle, and Dixxon finds one witch fighting another in her clearing. She runs in to help but gets knocked unconscious.

The winning witch hovers over Dixxon, preparing to kill her. A wolf jumps from above. He knocks the witch down, grabs Dixxon and runs off.

Scene - Ext. Mangy Mansion - Night
The wolf-creature takes Dixxon back to the porch of a tiny run-down shack—the outward appearance of Dixxon's mansion. Then the wolf howls loudly and runs back to the forest. Cat and Broom rush out.

Scene - Int. Mangy Mansion - Night
Broom carries Dixxon to a chair in front of the main fireplace. The inside of the "shack" is huge, but mildly run

down. A roaring fire lights up the entire downstairs. Dixxon relates her tale of witnessing a witch fight in the woods and then an animal saving her. Cat and Broom tell her she's had another dream. Dixxon falls asleep in front of the fire.

Beat 2 - Set Up the Inciting Incident

Scene - Int. Mangy Mansion - Next Morning
Morning activities around the inside of the mansion.

Scene - Ext. Road to Town - Day
Dixxon goes to school in a horse-drawn buggy.

Scene - Int. Brimstone Hill Schoolhouse - Day
Under Catholic voodoo headmaster Father Felixx LaFavroux's tutelage, school is about training to fight magical creatures.

Beat 3 - Inciting Incident

Scene - Ext. Brimstone Hill Schoolhouse - Day
Town boys tease an outcast boy. Dixxon tries to protect him and, using magic, accidentally kills an outcast girl. Dixxon's friend, Magnolia, cuts a deal with the outcast boy to take the blame for Dixxon.

Scene - Int. Brimstone Hill Schoolhouse: Father Fe-

Iixx's Office - Day

Town girls tell the priest about the incident and he resolves to hunt down the witch responsible and burn her.

Part 2 - Run For Your Life

Beat 4 - Reaction to the Inciting Incident

Scene - Ext. Prien Lake - Day

Dixxon flees along the lake back to her mansion.

Beat 5 - First Pinch Point - Introduce the evil force

Scene - Ext. Black Lake: Bile Island - Night

The Witch Council convenes. They discuss the coming full blue moon and what to do with Dixxon.

Beat 6 - Reaction to the First Pinch Point

Scene - Ext. Mangy Mansion - Day

A witch claiming to be Dixxon's aunt from the witch council shows up on the doorstep of the mansion.

Beat 7 - Lead Up to the Midpoint

Scene - Ext. Frasch Forest: Wolf Den - Day

Bane (the boy who got teased at school) and his mate, Amia, carry the dead carcass of Amia's best friend back to their pack leader, Haine. Haine puts a "hit" out on our hero, Dixxon.

Scene - Ext. Brimstone Hill Schoolhouse - Day
Back in town, the headmaster has Dixxon's friend, Magnolia, captive. He lets her go so they can follow her to Dixxon.

Scene - Ext. Frasch Forest - Day
A dwarf follows Magnolia to the forest. Magnolia meets with Bane and solidifies her deal.

Scene - Int. Mangy Mansion - Day
Dixxon is freaking out that her friend has been captured. She wants to go back and find her. She looks out the window and sees blue moon getting bluer each night. Then she hears wolves howl in the forest.

Scene - Ext. Prien Lake: Travel to Mangy Mansion - Day
Magnolia leaves the wolf, Bane, and goes to Dixxon's mansion. The dwarf follows her to the entrance.

Beat 8 - Midpoint

Scene - Int. Brimstone Hill Schoolhouse: Father Felixx's Office - Night
The dwarf goes back to town to tell about Magnolia meet-

ing the wolf and then going to Dixxon's "shack." When the dwarf leaves, Father Felixx speaks into his fireplace to an unseen person about Dixxon.

Scene - Ext. Along Prien Lake - Night
Townspeople walk along the lake with torches and crossbows.

Scene - Ext. Mangy Mansion - Night
Townspeople stand outside Dixxon's mansion and tell her to give herself up.

Scene - Int. Mangy Mansion - Night
Dixxon and her friends hover inside the mansion. Townspeople break into the mansion and a fight ensues. Dixxon's friend, Magnolia, is taken and her guardian broom gets broken. Dixxon escapes with Cat and Auntie.

Scene - Int. Mangy Mansion: Kitchen - Night
Townspeople find one of their girls lying dead in the mansion kitchen after the fight.

Scene - Ext. Frasch Forest: Camp - Night
Dixxon and Cat and Auntie have escaped and set up camp in the forest.

Scene - Ext. Frasch Forest: Burning Post - Night
Townspeople take Magnolia to the burning post inside the

forest. They light the fire and Magnolia screams and howls. The wolf pack howls back.

Scene - Ext. Frasch Forest: Camp - Night
Dixxon hears the howling and before Cat can stop her, she takes off through the swampy forest.

Scene - Ext. Frasch Forest: Burning Post - Night
Dixxon gets to the clearing just as the pack of wolves attack the townspeople and disappear into the forest with her friend, Magnolia.

Scene - Ext. Frasch Forest (Running) - Night
Dixxon follows the wolves through the forest.

Scene - Ext. Frasch Forest: Wolf Den - Night
By the time she catches up to them, Bane's mate is just about to kill Magnolia. Magnolia sees Dixxon and yells at her to leave. Bane sees her too and races at her to scare her away. Dixxon runs, but circles back to watch, too late to intervene. Bane's mate kills Magnolia. Dixxon flees.

Part 3 - Fight Back and Fail

Beat 9 - Reaction to the Midpoint

Scene - Ext. Frasch Forest: Camp - Night
Back at the forest camp, Dixxon's panicked and crying.

Cat tries to calm her down. Auntie Maxx informs them that they have to go back to the mansion. Cat agrees. Dixxon agrees as well.

Scene - Int. Mangy Mansion - Day
The mansion's a mess, but the townspeople are gone. Dixxon puts a protection spell around the mansion, but a mysterious white cat shows up on the doorstep and Black Cat lets her in. Dixxon repairs Broom, but something's "off" about him.

Beat 10 - Second Pinch Point - Re-introduce the evil force

Scene - Ext. Black Lake: Bile Island - Night
The Witch Council discusses and disagrees about killing Dixxon. Auntie Maxx reports to the Council through the fireplace in the mansion. "You have one day until the blue moon," the Council tells Auntie. "It has to be solved by then." (Ticking-clock reminder.)

Beat 11 - Reaction to the Second Pinch Point

Scene - Int. Mangy Mansion - Morning
White Cat saw Auntie talking into the fireplace and tries to convince Dixxon that she's up to no good. Dixxon's distracted, preparing to go to the forest and deal with the wolves.

Beat 12 - The Pre-Second Plot Point Lull

Scene - Int. Mangy Mansion: Kitchen - Day
Black Cat, White Cat, Broom and Dixxon end up in the kitchen around the cauldron. Black Cat and Broom ask Dixxon what she's going to do. She tells them that wolves have to pay for Magnolia's death. She leaves the kitchen to go to the forest after them. Black Cat, White Cat and Broom stare at the cauldron. "You think she's ready yet?" asks White Cat. Black Cat says, "She's almost there. . ."

Beat 13 - Lead Up to the Second Plot Point

Scene - Ext. Frasch Forest: Wolf Den - Night
Dixxon attacks the wolves but Bane's mate kicks her butt. Bane saves her again.

Scene - Ext. Mangy Mansion - Night
Bane takes Dixxon back to her mansion and is met by Black Cat, White Cat and Auntie. Bane growls at Auntie and she goes inside.

Scene - Int. Mangy Mansion - Night
Auntie watches Bane exchange words with Black and White Cat, nodding in agreement to whatever he's saying, and Auntie isn't pleased.

Scene - Ext. Frasch Forest: Wolf Den - Night

The Alpha, Haine, decrees that Bane has to leave the pack because he keeps going against orders. The pack turns against Bane. He runs off.

Beat 14 - Second Plot Point

Scene - Int. Mangy Mansion - Morning

Dixxon wakes up and the cats try to tell her about Auntie. Meanwhile Broom seems to be sticking much closer to Auntie Maxx. Cats inform Dixxon that Auntie Maxx is trying to kill her because she's the last white witch and at the next blue moon she has to save witchcraft! Also, the wolves will kill Bane when he returns to the forest. And White Cat is actually Magnolia from school and she only cut a deal with Bane to save Dixxon. Bane will die if Dixxon doesn't save him before the next full moon.

Part 4 - Climax

Beat 15 - Hero Accepts Reality

Scene - Ext. Prien Lake - Night

Dixxon goes to find Bane in the forest to save him from his pack. The frogs warn her that Bane has been captured by the priest and is staked to the witch burning post. They allude to how she has to sacrifice to become a white witch.

Scene - Ext. Frasch Forest: Burning Post - Night

Dixxon tries to save Bane and gets captured by the evil priest. It's almost the full blue moon—Dixxon's birthday. Auntie Maxx shows up and says that they have to kill Dixxon before she turns into the white witch.

Witch fight. Black Cat and White Cat show up to help—they turn into witches in battle. Auntie Maxx is too powerful and she and the priest capture them, too. As the priest and the townspeople are about to burn the "cats" and Dixxon, the moon turns full and her power increases and she escapes her bonds. Priest and Auntie threaten to kill cats and Bane. Dixxon saves them all by sacrificing herself to Auntie and priest. But that's how you become a true white witch—sacrifice at a blue moon. Priest lets cats go and takes Dixxon prisoner, but Auntie takes her instead.

Bane and cats escape into the forest.

Scene - Ext. Prien Lake: Shoreline to Mangy Mansion - Night

Auntie drags Dixxon back to the mansion to gloat and monologue.

Beat 16 - Climax Battle Scene

Scene - Int. Mangy Mansion: Kitchen - Night
Auntie taunts Dixxon, gloating and. . . Oh, what's in this cauldron? Dixxon makes up a lie about a potion that brings eternal youth or immortality. "Youth is wasted on the young. And it won't save you, Dixxon, last white witch indeed." Auntie Maxx sips from the cauldron. Choke, you treacherous . . . choke . . . and auntie melts down to goo and bursts into purple flame!

Beat 17 - New Equilibrium

Scene - Int. Mangy Mansion: Kitchen - Morning After Full Moon
Black Cat, White Cat, Dixxon and Broom are in kitchen chatting. Broom is acting strangely.

Scene - Ext. Black Lake: Bile Island - Night
Witch Council talks about how they hexed Broom as a spy.

Scene - Int. Brimstone Hill Schoolhouse: Father Felixx's Office - Night
The priest goes through the evil auntie's belongings—Broom smuggled them to him from Dixxon's kitchen—and finds a locket with a picture of his dead wife and a hidden picture of a baby.

Scene - Ext. Frasch Forest (Running) - Night

The pack is chasing Bane as we close the scene and the book.

OUTLINING SOFTWARE

Excel, a Word document, text document. . . There are all kinds of software programs out there that you can use to help you outline and keep track of your story's plot points, characters, descriptions and summaries, and/or story beats. By far the best one—my opinion, remember—for actual plot-point outlining is the tool that I use, Scrivener.

By putting my story's milestones right inside Scrivener, using the Four Part Story Structure filled in with beats to summarize my scenes, I create a roadmap I can follow to fill in the blanks of my story right inside the application that I'll be using to write.

Of course, it sounds easier than it is, but with a questionnaire-style, fill-in-the-blanks format, outlining and story structuring meld together to make things quicker once I start writing.

EXPANDING ON OUR BEAT SHEET

We've successfully created a working outline that we can use inside Scrivener. We have a story, themes, characters, backstories, vocabulary and a plot, and we have it all overlaying the Four Part Story Structure. We *could* simply dive in and begin writing to that outline—there's enough information, outline and details in our master spreadsheet and Scrivener outline to do that.

But in the next section, I'm going to show you how I expand that outline to a working summary Scrivener file that helps me push up my word count and, more importantly, detail my story further so I don't miss any plot holes.

As I went back through this outline for *Dixxon*, I realized that I hadn't defined my ticking-clock chronology well enough to keep the tension building and the stakes increasing as it got closer to the full moon. My outline helped me identify that and go back and fix it.

:: ACTION ITEM

Create a beat sheet for your story using the example we just did for Dixxon—A Teen Witch. **Coincidentally, there are 17 beats for that outline and they fit nicely inside the Four Part Story Structure.** That is to say they mesh up with the 17 stages in the monomyth I mentioned earlier.

In the Bonus Materials, there's a Scrivener file of this beat sheet for *Dixxon—Teen Witch* as an example. You can download it and see how I put all of these beats into

Scrivener as the starting point for Lise and me to write the novel.

13
EXAMPLE 4PSS OUTLINE

4PSS - BEYOND THE BEAT SHEET

Now, I'm going to show you the overlay Lise and I did for our *Dixxon* novella, plotting it to the Four Part Story Structure as an example of the way I expand my outline before filling in the story by writing it.

First, here are the summary exercise results of Lise and me talking over the Internet for three hours, brainstorming and outlining our *Dixxon* novella.

SUMMARY EXERCISE FOR DIXXON

I wanted to show you the exercise we ran through to kickstart our *Dixxon—Teen Witch* outline summary and master spreadsheet information.

Our theme

Evil is in the eye of the beholder.

Overarching theme for all books

If Dixxon doesn't continue to save the day, dark magic will take over and control everything—turn everyone into evil followers. Good versus evil in the midst of love.

What if?

What if the last white witch was to be "born" on her sixteenth birthday under a full blue moon? What if she was the last hope of saving magic and mankind from plunging into dark rule? And what if all she wanted to do was to find a boyfriend?

Locations

Brimstone Hill

One hundred years in the future, the world has reverted back to an early American puritan style of living. In Brimstone Hill, Louisiana, over five hundred years of voodoo superstition has melded with an oppressive Catholic zealotry to produce fearful, fierce and ferocious townspeople, bent on destroying magical creatures wherever they might be found. Magic and man . . . do not mix.

The Frasch Forest

The dark woods surrounding our town have magical and

monstrous creatures in them. Some have existed since the dawn of time as paranormal beings, and some of them genetically mutated—frogs—since the end of the industrial and technological age of the past.

SIDE NOTE:

Frogs are a good metaphor for humanity's destruction, as many scientists have tracked the declining global population of frog species as a precursor to an eventual environmental meltdown. This is part of that research I mentioned. So it makes ironic sense that their job is to croak out warnings.

The Mangy Mansion

The Mangy Mansion is the witch safe house for white witches just before they turn 16. It's a dark, creepy and mysterious "fun" house.

The Black Lake

The Witch Council convenes in the center of Black Lake on Bile Island. The swamps surrounding Bile Island are filled with all manner of biting creatures—alligators, snakes and "bats" to name a few.

Society

In the aftermath of a societal meltdown that few remember but none want to repeat, humanity has resurrected to a world without electricity, solely powered by steam and heated by burning wood for fuel. Houses are heated with fireplaces again and lit with candles at night.

Religion

School is taught in churches again and religion rules over fearful and faithful townspeople. Father Felixx LaFavroux leads his flock in the pursuit and destruction of magical creatures. "Dazzling devils of the darkness," he calls them in sermons, "that must be put to death!"

Our world's style

The world is iron and gray. The clothing is black and white and shades of gray, accentuated by shades of red, purple and green. It's a futuristic cross between steam punk and puritan fashion. Girls wear white lace-covered shirts up to their necks and the boys wear gray trousers and black shirts, sprinkled with just enough trinketry to make them fashionable. "Puritan punk," we call it.

The entire town is reminiscent of an East Coast U.S. settlement in the 1500s-1600s that, instead of practicing devout Catholicism, sacrifices magical animals—witches, werewolves and magic cats—to appease God.

The stakes

In the magical world, dark purple, red and green mist wafts from boiling cauldrons of conjuring craft. The witches of old reign over the magical kingdom with one rule—magic and mankind must not mix. But this delicate balance between mortals and magic has been upset before and now the dark Witch Council has put out an edict that mankind must be exterminated before he once again destroys the earth. There's only one thing standing in their way.

Enter our hero

Every blue moon—an event as rare as what it produces—a white witch is born through sacrifice. If she's allowed to survive, the balance between dark and light—magic and man—will be restored and the world will go on as it has. Magic will remain hidden in the darkness and man will continue to rule the day, leaving magic and its creatures to prowl the night and forest.

Dixxon must figure out who she is before the next full moon or the worlds of magic and man will be lost from the light . . . forever.

Love interest

The young werewolf, Bane, has saved Dixxon's soup more times than she knows about, but if the town ever finds out who he really is. . . Well, burned or beaten to death? It's not as bad as what Dixxon might do if she ever finds out what he did to her best friend.

Sidekicks

Black Cat is Dixxon's "Yoda."
The Mangy Mansion is alive.
Broom is the housekeeper that takes care of the house.
Fairy godmother Magnolia is Dixxon's friend at school.

Villains

Haine, the Alpha Werewolf (modeled on Derek's uncle from *Teen Wolf*), names all the other werewolves. They used to be slaves to witches (a la the movie *Underworld*). The alpha, Haine, just took over the wolves and became their master.

Dark Witch Council thinks mankind can't be saved (they'll turn magic against the realms). They send Auntie Maxxine is to deal with Dixxon.

Weapons

Humans have steam-powered crossbows that shoot repeating silver bolts—arrows. The arrows burst into flames on impact.

Witches have magical potions and spells. Werewolves have fangs and shapeshifting. Cats have claws and shift to feline witches in a fight.

PART 1 - WHY DO I CARE?

PURPOSE OF PART 1

The main question you must ask yourself in Part 1 is "Have I made my reader care about my hero and his or her friends?"

The goals for Part 1 are to hook your reader, give them a hero to relate to and root for, introduce them to a strange new world that you've created, and then set them on an unavoidable quest.

You're going to do this with a strong opening scene, a quick hook event, some situational and revealing world-building scenes, and then an inciting incident that will change your hero's world forever.

Let's do it!

Opening Scene

Where and when does your story take place?

Your opening scene is the first chance you get to introduce your reader to your world. You'll want to start them somewhere interesting.

Think about it: If you toured someone through your house, would you start at the closet? Probably not. You'd most likely take them right to your favorite room to show it off.

Find a place in your world that you love and start your reader there. You don't have to introduce your hero, though it's a great place to start, but something cool and maybe even a little mysterious early on, helps a reader settle in for a fun ride.

Example in our own little story

Fifteen years ago, in the depths of the swampy Frasch Forest, the townspeople, led by the local Catholic voodoo priest, are going to burn a woman they believe is a witch.

A good witch is racing through the forest to save her. He knows the woman isn't a witch. Just as he's about to burst into the burning clearing, a dark witch grabs him from behind and stops him. She forces him to watch while the mortal woman burns at the stake, screaming for him to save her.

The dark witch banishes the good witch. Informs him that the Witch Council has decreed he's never allowed to return to the kingdom of witches, the Black Lake.

Awaken from the dream

Our teen hero, Dixxon, is a young witch living in her Mangy Mansion, quietly and happily going about the everyday life that she knows.

She wakes up from the dream of the woman being burned at the stake. It's the middle of the night and she's yelling for her guardians, Cat and Broom. When they get to her, they tell her she's had another nightmare. The dreams are getting worse as it approaches Dixxon's sixteenth birthday—the next full moon.

Dixxon tells Cat that she needs to go for a walk in the moonlight to calm her nerves. Cat warns against going out in the dark, because magical creatures are becoming more restless as the full moon approaches. Dixxon is out the door before he can stop her.

Results

We've done a couple of things: Introduced our reader to the dark forest, magic, witch burning, dark witches with treacherous hearts, and we've banished someone from his own "tribe" of people. We've also established that our hero's a witch who will turn sixteen at the next full moon.

That's a lot of world building and setup. We've got our reader interested in the "bait," now let's hook them and reel them into the boat.

THE HOOK

What early event enthralls and captivates your audience's attention?

The hook is an irresistible event that happens early on to "hook" your reader into your story. Hooks are exciting and fun scenes, but often lack the context of the story to give them meaning to the reader. They're riddles to be solved as you unravel the mystery in your book.

In fact, our little opening witch-burning scenes are a pretty good hook, but let's pile on a little more—really pull in our reader.

Example:

Dixxon likes to roam the woods at night to calm herself. All witches love the night. The shores of Prien Lake are pitch black, but witches see in the dark as well as if it were day.

The edges of the lake teem with frogs. They speak in ominous riddles, and Dixxon sings little rhymes back. The songs are reminiscent of spells.

The light is bright when day is night
For witches right and things that bite
And voodoo too sees bright and blue
But there's none for me—[she picks two weeds]—*and two for you* (foreshadowing the cauldron and the two dead bodies that it will cause)

Dixxon enters the dark Frasch Forest, headed to her favorite clearing where she watches the moon in awe and fascination. A howling wolf—music to her ears—sounds stranger this night.

The howling turns to screeching and then scuffle and then battle, and Dixxon runs and finds one witch fighting another in a small clearing.

She tries to help but gets blasted with a spell and knocked unconscious before getting a good look at either one of them.

The winning witch looms over Dixxon's unconscious body. She's going to kill her.

A wolf—too big to be a normal one—jumps from above to stop the witch from killing Dixxon. He knocks the witch down, grabs Dixxon and runs off.

The wolf-creature takes Dixxon back to the porch of a tiny run-down shack—the outward appearance of Dixxon's Mangy Mansion. Then it howls loudly and runs back to the forest.

Cat and Broom rush out and Broom carries Dixxon to a chair in front of the main fireplace. The inside of the "shack" is insanely huge, but mildly run down. A roaring fire lights up the entire downstairs in orange flickers. Cat conjures a cup of tea from the kitchen.

Dixxon relates her tale of witnessing a witch fight in the woods and then an animal saving her.

Cat and Broom tell her she's had another dream, because her birthday is coming.

Dixxon falls asleep in front of the fire.

Results:

Here's what we've done. A lot more world introduction and an event—two witches fighting in the woods—that lacks context, but is itself a little mini-mystery we'll unravel later.

And another thing: We've established a ticking clock, though we don't know its consequences yet. That ticking clock? The next full moon and Dixxon's birthday. It's getting clearer that there'll be some changes in 30 days. Big changes.

SETTING UP THE INCITING INCIDENT SCENES

How will you introduce your readers to the new world they now find themselves in? And then how will you set up the fact that you're going to change that world for your hero . . . forever?

If Part 1 is all about introductions and intrigue, then it's also about setting up the stakes for your hero's eventual quest. What does the hero and/or the world he or she lives in stand to gain if your hero undertakes the quest? What will they all lose if he or she doesn't?

How to deliver stakes to your reader

Using expositional information is one way to tell your reader about consequences. Simply lay it all out in gory detail for them from the narrator's point of view. Give them everything they need to know to understand what's happened to and in the world—real or imagined—up to that point.

Or . . . you could slowly introduce them to that world and its peril through the thoughts, dialogue and actions of its inhabitants.

I like the second one.

Everything in the "lead up to the inciting incident" scenes builds our hero's world. The setting, the stakes and the mystery unravels slowly as we introduce our readers to a world as yet unfamiliar to them.

We foreshadow things to come by dripping seemingly incidental information into scenes. Sideways views of surroundings, tiny events or objects that may make no sense until later. And we slowly unfold the time, place and society that our new world is built around.

Dixxonland

Dixxon awakens the next morning, still sitting in the chair in front of the crackling fire. She looks in her hand at the weeds she picked the night before and then goes to the kitchen.

In the kitchen, a big iron pot bubbles slowly and steams above a round kitchen fire pit. Dixxon drops in the weeds and purple and green mist billow from the cauldron. (The cauldron's actually a very important part of our story, but we just want to hint at it this early on.)

Dixxon comes out of the kitchen, drinking tea and munching a biscuit, to a nervous and edgy Cat and Broom. "Off to school?" they ask.

"Yes," Dixxon says. "And before you two start, I'm always careful." At which point, Dixxon "poofs" the plate that her biscuit was on. It disappears, and we hear it break in the kitchen (foreshadowing Dixxon's magical mistake that actually starts her quest). She giggles, shrugs and heads out the front door.

Outside is a hapless horse and battered buggy, waiting to take her to town to attend school. A dark but well-dressed man in a long black wool coat and tall black top hat sits as her driver. We never see his face. His boots are old and leather-laced and he has dingy white gloves on. "Nice shirt, mum," he says.

"Don't be silly," says Dixxon, "you know they only allow white lace for girls." Dixxon tugs at the tight collar of her "puritan punk" shirt. "Uncomfortable matters not." When Dixxon steps into the carriage, we see her tall black boots laced to perfection, and her long gray skirt adorned with a red sash for a belt—the only color on her otherwise earth-toned outfit.

Townland

Dixxon arrives at school in Brimstone Hill with all the other children. The only thing that stands out is the clique of girls who laugh and scoff at Dixxon, themselves having arrived in carriages just slightly better and dressed slightly more "fashionably" than their fellow classmates. Yet, in fact, there are those kids, the outcasts, who are even less well-dressed than Dixxon and her only friend at school, Magnolia.

The outcasts are rough and raw-looking, and eye everyone with upturned lips and half smiles. But one in particular pays close attention to Dixxon. She smiles at him and he hesitatingly smiles back. (We're hinting along the lines of *Twilight* here.)

By the time the first break in the school arrives, we've met the local Catholic voodoo priest, who also happens to be the town's schoolmaster. When he speaks of dark witchcraft and magic and burning witches at the stake to appease a God who's angry at humanity for the ruin they've caused, Dixxon's blood runs cold.

Never again will the priests of the future allow man to destroy his own world, and never again will man share that world with the likes of the wolves and witches of the Frasch Forest and the Black Lake. Eradication is the only way that mankind will survive!

School is more like training to fight evil creatures. The priest teaches the class about silver arrows that ignite on impact, shot from crossbows with rotating bolts powered by small super-steam turbine engines. We're no longer in a puritan world, the reader discovers; we're in a post-apocalyptic era 100 years in the future, rebuilt on steam and heated and lit with fire.

During the training, we're shown that the outcasts are nervous about the silver arrows and Dixxon and her friend are equally apprehensive about the fact that they catch fire due to a brimstone coating that's been mined from the local sulphur deposits. The mine was resurrected from its former glory in the 1940s.

We've set up the confrontation that will inevitably follow, based around fire and silver and witches and—what are these "outcast" kids, anyway? They're a bit "mongrel"-feeling.

QUICK TIP:

Many people find it difficult to get the word count necessary for a full-length novel—50,000-100,000 words. An outline helps break that number down into manageable bite-sized chunks that you can write as scenes with a single purpose—set up the next scene in the sequence.

Results:

In just writing the explanations and examples for our opening scene, hook, and lead-up scenes to our inciting incident, we've put down 2,000+ words. Once we actually fill in the details of those scenes, they'll most likely double and probably triple. That'll end up being roughly 6,000 words and we haven't even talked about the inciting incident.

Extend that out to four parts and we have 24,000 words. I like math. It helps to "chunk" things down to manageable smaller bites.

THE INCITING INCIDENT

Until now, our hero has lived in her nicely understood world with her mechanisms to hide and run under the radar, well in place. Dixxon's world is understood to her and she's able to move through it easily. She likes it and can survive there. All that's about to change. Because if it didn't, there'd be no story.

To set our hero on a journey and quest of self-discovery and challenge them to grow beyond their nice tidy little belief system and world, we have to set some event upon them that they can't escape or avoid. Sometimes it's nice if that event was a complete accident. But one thing's for sure: It upsets the balance of their everyday life forever from that point forward.

Otherwise known as the First Plot Point

For our Dixxon, there's no time to wonder about it, because the Maplewood kids, from the section of town where the wealthy and privileged live, are harassing Dixxon and her friend. One of the outcast boys—the one always eyeing Dixxon—comes to her aid only to find himself at the bottom of a pile of Maplewood boys. He finally ends up being threatened with a silver arrow that one of those boys has taken from class training.

Seeing the fear on the outcast boy's face, Dixxon panics and does what Cat and Broom have told her never to do —she uses magic to stop the town boys. But since she's desperate and the impending full moon has her powers growing, she accidentally "black-crafts" one of the outcast girls, killing her. And the only one who saw her do it was the boy she was trying to save, Bane.

The town girls turn and see Dixxon and her friend, Magnolia, standing there and accuse them both of being witches. Magnolia moves to protect Dixxon, but Bane— the outcast boy Dixxon saved—tells them both to run!

Scared and confused, Dixxon runs.

Results:

We've successfully got our hero's apple cart upturned, forcing her to run for her life—Part 1's overarching purpose. Our hero has two choices: run for her life or get caught and burned as a witch. She runs, and we've exited Part 1 of our story doing what we needed to.

Now, our reader is intrigued about the mysteries we've introduced, informed about the world and what's at stake for everyone in it, and now they want to find out what will happen to "their" hero, Dixxon. The only way to do that is to read Part 2.

Congratulations. That was the purpose of Part 1—get your reader to Part 2.

QUICK TIP:

You see where I'm going with this, right? Despite the infinite amount of resources available, championing style and panache and feel and other fornicated felicities, what you really need as a new author is the understanding that storytelling, at its core, is selling.

Storytelling is story-selling

Your book cover and title must "sell" a reader to look at your summary, your summary must sell them on opening the front cover, the opening scene must sell them on reading the next one and the hook, and then to the inciting incident and then on to all the parts of your novel. Ultimately selling them to pay the real cost to them of reading your novel—10+ hours of their lives reading your story.

Of course your story has to be decent to do all of that, but it must also be decent at the right points in an increasingly overstimulated reader's mind. This is the reason that epic books sell better as three-hour movies and short Kindle books perform so well. Attention span and the opportunity cost of time.

But Darth, I'm an artist.
There's a reason they put the word "starving" in front of that.

:: ACTION ITEM

Sit down and quickly summarize your way through Part 1 of your book. Write a couple sentences for each of these: your opening scene, your hook, a few scenes of world-building—scene, setting and stakes—and an inciting incident, whose purpose is to set your hero on their quest.

Remember, this is your document, so it's okay if you leave gaps in it. The main thing is, you want to make sure you touch on all the major milestones of the Four Part Story Structure. If you do that, you're free to write your story any way you want in between those milestones as long as your hero arrives at each one on time.

PART 2 - WHY DO I FEAR?

PURPOSE OF PART 2 - RUN FOR YOUR LIFE

Ask yourself, why would I fear for someone's safety? Then you need to weave that into your hero's story outline.

Hopefully, in Part 1 we've made our hero likable enough that the reader can empathize with them. Now, the purpose of Part 2 is for the hero to run for their lives. They have to be clueless and ineffective at fixing anything. No matter what he or she tries, our hero can't seem to figure out what's going on.

But by the end of Part 2, our hero *does* figure out, at least partially, what they're up against. And we want our reader to fear for them as they go through that process—the "run for your life" phase.

Squarely at the end of Part 2, we want our hero to turn from frightened and feeble to a man or woman—boy or girl—on a mission to get justice or the emotional equivalent. Turn and win the girl or guy, resolve to fight the bad guys. . .

In short, Luke has to grab his lightsaber and go after Darth Vader at the end of Part 2. Of course in Part 3, Darth Vader's gonna cut off Luke's hand, but let's not get ahead of ourselves.

REACTION TO THE INCITING INCIDENT

Whatever happens at your first plot point (inciting incident), the beginning of Part 2 is your hero's reaction to it—run, scared for his or her life!

Dixxon runs. She ends up safely back inside her "shack" with Cat and Broom. She's freaking out about being a witch, because she just accidentally killed one of the outcast girls in town. But her friend, Magnolia, hasn't shown up yet and she wants to go back and get her.

Cat and Broom say that's out of the question because they know the consequences of Dixxon having been discovered. This is now the core of their job—protect the last white witch.

With the next full moon—the once in a blue moon—just around the corner, Cat and Broom are sure that the Witch Council will be sending a representative to help them get Dixxon through the ordeal.

[A knock at the door] That'll be her now.

QUICK TIP:

Knocks at the door, phones ringing, a crack of thunder—literal interruptions in your story—are good places to switch scenes, locations and perspective. Thrust your reader sideways and leave them with a little mini-cliffhanger to wonder about until you bring them back.

Think about how many times the secret in a story was just about to be revealed when some opportune interruption kept the hero from hearing the truth . . . too early in the story, I might add. This is why we sit in a movie and yell at the screen, "Just tell her that her boyfriend cheated on her with her father, already!"

But if that revelation came out too early, the story would rocket to an end too quickly. That line above would be a second plot point revelation.

Just in case you think that line above is hokey or icky, it's the entire plot point two reveal of the movie *White Bird in a Blizzard*.

FIRST PINCH POINT

Pinch points are the places where you allude to the evil force. They represent a sprinkle of sinister resistance that the hero will most likely not understand until it's almost too late. They serve to introduce the dark forces that will haunt the hero throughout his or her journey.

We let the reader see the evil force directly, not filtered through the hero's eyes. This is the evil plot that threatens our hero, though it's as yet unclear to him or her. The first pinch point is merely a glimpse at that evil, not a full accounting of the danger.

Witchland—the Witch Council

Across Prien Lake, south through the dark Frasch Forest and down the 'ol Kalkashoo River to the deepest darkest part of the bayou. . . Right before the river releases its muddy silt into the Gulf of what used to be Mexico, the mysterious and murderous Black Lake rests like a dark hole to nowhere. In the middle of that lake, surrounded by swamp so thick and creatures so treacherous that it can only be reached by someone who's been there before, lies the cursed Bile Island.

Each 100 years, Bile Island hosts dark and light witches from all over the realms in a gathering of greatness. The purpose of this meeting is to discuss the state of magic in the world and ensure its survival . . . by any means necessary.

For thousands of years the meeting has been about balance, but this millennium the whispers are of extinction . . . and what's to be done about it. At this gathering, dark and light witches will discuss the next white witch, the wolf "problem" and the future "health" of humanity. And it seems that there's a disagreement among the Council as to whether this next white witch will save them . . . or get them all killed.

There's mention of an answer to that question, already on its way to assess the situation and report back. But the sideways glances and looks out of the corners of eyes tells us that whether that's all the truth there is to it, remains to be seen.

Then we leave the pinch point with another mystery to solve, further consequences to ponder, and more apprehension for our uninformed hero.

REACTION TO FIRST PINCH POINT

Where the reaction to the first plot point—the inciting incident—ended with Dixxon running and then a knock at the door, after the first pinch point, the reaction will still be one of bewilderment. Our hero simply isn't ready to understand everything and start making decisions just yet. Rest assured by the end of Part 2 he or she will have all the information they need and a renewed purpose to turn and start defending themselves.

Back in Dixxonland

Cat opens the front "door"—the tiny broken-down shack on the shores of Prien Lake—of the Mangy Mansion and comes whisker to tall, brown boot ankle with none other than Maxxine Levine, Dixxon's "auntie."

Cat knows that "auntie" stuff is cat litter—all witches are aunts and uncles to all other witches. Because none of them are allowed to marry or mate with any being other than a witch. In the history of all craft conjurers, there's only been one witch to break that rule . . . and he's dead.

Cat and Broom are cautious, but if the Witch Council has sent this one to help, she must be okay.

After some introductions and niceties, Auntie "Maxx" settles into the mansion.

LEAD UP TO THE MIDPOINT

Several scenes will involve getting our hero to her midpoint "understanding."

At the middle of Part 2, we start to slowly move the hero towards understanding what he or she is up against. In our story, there are several groups of characters whom we have to bring along with us on that trip. So now we're going to switch to the outcast boy who almost got killed at school, Bane.

On to Wolfland

Deep in the dark and swampy Frasch Forest, Bane and his mate, Amia, carry the dead carcass of Amia's best friend back to their pack leader, Haine. Haine is himself a mystery of sorts and as the leader of this pack of werewolves, it's up to him to pass judgment on the one who killed one of his pack. But when Haine asks who the responsible party is, Bane lies and says it was Dixxon's friend, Magnolia.

Bane and Amia dispute this—she can smell something on him—but he manages to convince Haine that it was Magnolia who black-casted Amia's dead friend and Haine issues an order that Bane and Amia must go and kill Magnolia.

Meanwhile, in Townland. . .

And this is how story-pacing goes—at logical conclusion points to scenes and/or lines of your plot, you can switch to follow secondary story lines or other characters and locations by ending the chapter and starting a new one at a new location.

The reason Dixxon didn't see her friend escape is because the girl didn't—the voodoo priest, Felixx LaFavroux, got her. But he's crafty and he knows that to find a witch you must follow a witch. So he tells the town boys to let her go and secretly has one of the town dwarves follow the girl. (The dwarf humans have been relegated to spies for the church. And this one needs to find Dixxon, so they can burn her and Magnolia.)

Driving to the middle

All of this leads up to the midpoint scenes, taking our reader inevitably towards a peak event at the middle of the story. It's there that our hero will come face to face with the death of some delusion, person, their own idealism, or some other understanding that will leave them resolved to fight back against the evil that caused that event.

QUICK TIP:

For those of you who write romance or humor, villains take all shapes and forms, but make no mistake, there is an "evil" or resisting force in romance and comedies, just as there is in a thriller. For instance, in *The Big Lebowski*, the evil force of the rich man searching for his money takes the place of an evil villain. And in *As Good As It Gets*, Jack Nicholson is plagued by the injury-prone neighbor, Greg Kinnear, getting in his way of trying to woo Helen Hunt. "Evil" is a term for an obstacle that the hero must overcome.

Back to our dwarf spy

The dwarf follows Magnolia, but she doesn't head straight to Dixxon. Instead Magnolia meets secretly with the outcast boy, Bane, in the Frasch Forest. And lo and behold, as seen through the eyes of the dwarf, the outcast boy is a werewolf. To the dwarf, it looks like he'll be well rewarded, because the townspeople are going to have a wolf and two witches to burn at the stake. (We're upping the stakes here.)

Dixxonland

While all this is going on, Dixxon is scared and freaking out to Cat and Broom and the newly arrived Auntie Maxx. She just knows her friend will be burned for being mistaken for a witch. In reality, Magnolia is Dixxon's fairy godmother, a protective witch, sent to keep Dixxon safe at school when she's away from the safety of the Mangy Mansion.

Dixxon wants to leave and save Magnolia, but Cat and

Broom won't let her. Despite this, Auntie keeps trying to help Dixxon leave for some reason.

The blue moon gets bluer the closer to the next full moon we get, and that night Dixxon sneaks out. She walks the shores of Prien Lake and hears the wolf pack howling. The frogs warn her not to get burned. (Foreshadowing the townspeople coming to get her.)

Wolf-forest land

After Magnolia and Bane meet, the dwarf follows Magnolia to Dixxon's run-down shack—the secret entrance to the Mangy Mansion—her witch lair.

Results:

And now we've set up the middle of our story. The tension is up, there are mysteries and consequences looming, our hero is freaking out—she has friends in danger—and the bad guys know where she is. The next thing that happens won't be good!

MIDPOINT

The death of something for our hero—delusions, body, soul . . . or a friend, maybe? The midpoint steels the hero's resolve—turns him or her to fight instead of run.

Our hero finally understands the dangers they face and comes to the realization that running from trouble . . . won't fix anything.

Our hero must meet face to face with the truth of what's chasing them. In short, they've figured things out at the end of Part 2. Or so he or she thinks. . .

Townland

The dwarf goes back to town to tell Father Felixx about Magnolia meeting a wolf and then going to Dixxon's shack.

The priest speaks secretly into his own fireplace to an unknown person. He says we have to kill her.

Priest and townspeople take torches and pitchforks and walk along Prien Lake towards the shack. The frogs are croaking out warnings about fire and brimstone, but humans can't understand it.

Dixxonland

Father Felixx and the torch-wielding townspeople stand outside the shack entrance to the Mangy Mansion and yell to Dixxon to give herself and her witch friend up . . . or they'll burn the place down.

Cat and Broom and Dixxon and Auntie Maxx all hover inside. Cat is confident that humans can't get in—he has a protection spell on the shack.

Town girls and boys are shouting, "Burn it down!" but Father Felixx wants to face the witches, not anonymously burn them. He wants to look the Black Lake's precious white witch in the eyes before he burns their savior to death.

Somehow, the priest breaks through Cat's protection spell and the townspeople go into the shack and find themselves inside the Mangy Mansion.

A fight ensues, but Auntie can't use her magic—curious—and Dixxon isn't powerful enough yet. So Auntie and Cat and Broom and Dixxon must escape through a secret passageway in the Mansion, but the townspeople take fairy godmother Magnolia hostage again.

In the melee, Broom gets broken in half and a town girl goes into the kitchen. She's found dead later by the other townspeople. (Foreshadowing the ending of the book.)

Frasch Forestland

Our hero and her sidekicks and Auntie have escaped and

set up camp in the Frasch Forest in a run-down, barely-above-water, two-story shack in the flooded cypress trees. "What do we do now?"

Frasch Forestland-the Burning Post

Townspeople take Magnolia to the burning post—the same one where our opening-scene woman was burned—just inside the Frasch Forest. Father Felixx's plan is to lure Dixxon, and if he can the wolf, with Magnolia's screams.

They light the fire and Magnolia closes her eyes and starts screaming, but it's more like howling.

The wolf pack in the forest howls back. Our hero's camp hears the howling and before Cat can stop her, Dixxon takes off through the swamp.

Dixxon gets to the clearing just as the pack of wolves attack the townspeople and take Magnolia from the burning post. The townspeople fight briefly but soon flee, despite Father Felixx's attempts to stop them. Then the wolves disappear into the forest, carrying Magnolia.

Dixxon follows the wolves, barely keeping pace. By the time she catches up to them, Bane's mate is just about to kill Magnolia.

Magnolia sees Dixxon and yells at her to leave. Bane turns and sees her too and he races at Dixxon, snarling to scare her away. Dixxon runs, but circles back.

Magnolia is killed in a fiery burst of light and Dixxon flees back to her camp in the forest.

Results:

And our hero has lost her only friend at school and now has a reason to hate the townspeople and the wolves enough that she's going to fight back against them both. And that drops us right at the beginning of Part 3.

PART 3 - WHY DO I SCREAM?

WISK

(we haven't had one of these in a while)

"In the ashes of failure . . . lay the seeds of success." (It's hard to be cynical and sarcastic all the time.)

PURPOSE OF PART 3 - FIGHT BACK AND FAIL

The purpose of Part 3 is for your hero to go from wanderer to warrior. After everything that's happened, they're no longer afraid enough to run; now they have the incentive and enough information to garner the courage to fight back. There are several scenes and milestones that we can write as goal lines to take our hero through that process.

But by the end of Part 3, just when it looks like they might win the day, we're gonna rip the wool off their eyes again at the second plot point, throwing our hero for another loop, but also providing them just enough further information to now, really, finally . . . defeat the bad guys.

REACTION TO THE MIDPOINT

What would happen if our hero lost something or someone irreplaceable? Would it finally wake them up enough to fight back in Part 3?

If all your hero wants is to get together with a certain person, at your midpoint, that possibility got seemingly lost forever. And that direction-changing event should lead you and your reader to ask yourselves one simple question: "What's he or she gonna do about that?" Because they clearly have to do something . . . something big.

In our own little story

If all Dixxon wanted was to have had parents, the closest she's come to that is her best friend at school, Magnolia. And at the midpoint . . . we killed her. She's going to do something about that.

Back at Dixxon's Forestland Camp

Dixxon is panicked and crying, and Cat's trying to calm her down, but he may know more than he's saying. And Auntie Maxx—for her escalating strange behavior, trying to get Dixxon alone—informs them that they have to go back to the mansion. Cat agrees—Broom's broken back there anyway. Dixxon, strangely, agrees as well. She needs something in the mansion to avenge her dead friend.

Back at the Mansion

The Mangy Mansion's a mess, but the townspeople are gone. Strange. . .

Dixxon has learned a little something about magic in her fifteen years, and she puts her own protection spell around the mansion. But a mysterious white cat shows up on the doorstep and Dixxon's own black cat lets her in.

Dixxon repairs Broom, but something's "off" about him. And our hero's back in her stronghold, plotting something in retaliation. Just where we want her.

SECOND PINCH POINT

Remember that evil force? About five-eighths of the way into your story, we're going to revisit that force.

When we re-introduce the evil villains, they'll be more ominous and threatening than they were at the first pinch point. And this time we'll know our hero is in some serious trouble.

At this point, we add a little more mystery and another little tidbit of information. Increasingly ominous overtones are the stuff of the second pinch. And the bad guys . . . get badder.

Witch Council-land—Black Lake

The Witch Council—both dark and light sides—are now concerned for the future of magic. There's discussion and disagreement about killing Dixxon. And Auntie Maxx—witch assassin "cleaner" that she's starting to look like—reports to the Council through the fireplace in the mansion.

The Witch Counsel asks why Dixxon hasn't been dealt with. "I haven't been able to get her alone. The cats are in my way . . . and Broom—" The Witch Council tells Auntie Maxx that Broom's been dealt with. What?

"You have two days until the blue moon," the Council tells Auntie. "It has to be resolved by then."

Results:

We show that the Witch Council has now turned to murderous actions, and we reintroduce the ticking clock of the blue moon coming.

REACTION TO SECOND PINCH POINT

Who saw the evil villains? Our reader? A character? Our hero?

Your hero may not know the true depths of the plot against him or her, but showing your reader the evil force up close and in gory detail has consequences. Someone will be affected—someone has to react to the event.

Dixxonland—the next morning

White Cat saw Auntie talking into the fireplace but didn't hear what she was saying. And come to think of it, Black Cat seems to remember Auntie disappearing while they were hiding in the swamp.

White Cat tries to convince Dixxon of this. Black Cat supports her—White Cat is a she? Hmmm...

Dixxon's in denial and distracted, preparing to go to the forest and deal with the wolves. "I don't care who she was talking to."

At some point, Black Cat, White Cat, Broom and Dixxon end up in the kitchen.

And now we all have to take a deep breath.

THE LULL

The lull is the calm before the storm, that uncomfortable

silence right before everyone whips out their guns and starts shooting. It's the point where the love triangle members all arrive at the punchbowl at the wedding at the same time and each of them only knows two-thirds of the story—theirs.

And in the lull we slip in a little tiny bit of information about the entire story. A tasty morsel a reader might miss, but gets wide-eyed later when we reveal it in context.

In our own little story

In the kitchen—around the cauldron—Black Cat, White Cat, Broom and Dixxon are talking casually. They ask Dixxon what she's going to do. She tells them that someone has to pay for Magnolia's death. White Cat and Black Cat exchange glances, but remain silent—Dixxon's gotta figure things out on her own.

Explanation:

If you ever notice yourself talking to your TV screen during the middle of a movie at a character who's being seemingly stupid—"Why don't you just tell her the truth and end all this secrecy?"

Disregard that it would end the story for everyone to just tell the truth all the time; oftentimes, what's happening only makes sense to the motivation of the character withholding that information.

Hero has to learn the hard way.

White and Black Cat could tell Dixxon that White Cat is actually the resurrected Magnolia, who was herself actually Jaxxine White, a fairy godmother—witch—who was charged with Dixxon's off-mansion security. But if you're going to become the most powerful witch there ever was, the last white witch, you're going to have to learn some things and go through some trials on your own.

Would Yoda or Obi-wan simply step in and tell Luke that Darth Vader is his father? I think not. How would Luke grow and gain by being handheld (yes, pun intended) through his own metamorphosis into a Jedi master? For that reason, a mentor—the cats—have to let little Dixxon fend for herself. In short, she's gotta grow up the way we all do. So, in the immortal words of Bad Cop in *The Lego Movie*, "They took the hard way."

Dixxon believes the wolves killed her friend Magnolia. She leaves the kitchen to go to the forest after them. Black Cat and White Cat and Broom stare at the cauldron. It's puffing purple smoke.

"This was your deal with the bog-dog beta?"

"So it would seem. . ."
"I hope you know what you're doing."
"So do I."

They continue to stare at the cauldron.

"You think she's ready yet?" asks White Cat. (This could mean Dixxon or whatever's brewing in that cauldron. Deliciously vague.)
"She's almost there. . ."

Results:

Now you've really got your reader ready for some action. You've hinted and made your hero run for their lives. You've showed your reader the dark force and left just enough out of the story that they don't quite know exactly what's going on. And now, you've sent your hero to deal with the "bad guys."

LEAD UP TO SECOND PLOT POINT

What earth-shattering, life-altering event will you unleash . . . again as your second plot point? Because that's what it is.

By the end of Part 2, our hero has finally gotten a handle on the evil that's stalking them. And in the first half of Part

3 we've successfully steeled the resolve of our hero to take that understanding and go deal with that evil. Now, at the end of Part 3, we're gonna show them that they don't even know the half of the trouble they're in.

The second plot point—rip the wool off of our little lamb hero's eyes . . . again! And we use a few scenes to position the hero in the right place where we can deliver that blow for maximum effect.

Forestland

Dixxon goes to cast magic and attack the wolves, but she's not powerful enough to defeat them and Bane's mate kicks her butt. But for his own reasons, though it's getting more obvious that he's got a thing for Dixxon, Bane saves her again, dragging her out of the forest. (We foreshadowed this at the very beginning of our story—saving her butt, dragging her from danger.)

Bane takes her back to the Mangy Mansion and is met by Black Cat and White Cat and Auntie. Bane growls at Auntie and she goes inside.

He exchanges words that we see only through Auntie's eyes, watching from a window above them. Bane and the cats nod in agreement to whatever they are saying and Auntie is not pleased.

Back in Wolfland

The Alpha decrees that Bane has to leave the pack because he keeps going against orders. Bane's mate is none too happy and agrees that Bane needs to be dealt with. The pack turns against Bane. He runs off.

Results:

We've got our hero completely set up to make a life-changing discovery, and now all we need to do is make the reader think they know exactly what that discovery is and what it will mean . . . then we need to jerk them sideways once we unleash the "real" revelation.

I know, it's a lot of moving parts. But think about if you were a pantser simply making this up as you went along. You would go nuts trying to get everyone queued up and in the right positions when the bombs drop. It's a good thing we know Four Part Story Structure and we're writing an outline to it, isn't it?

SECOND PLOT POINT

About three-quarters of the way through your story, you're going to unleash your second plot point bombshell and send your hero into the final battle of your novel—Part 4.

To do that, you might simultaneously have them get their butt kicked just as they figure out the reality of the situation.

This is where, if your hero has to kill someone to save the day, guess who that'll be? Their father.

"Luke, I am your father." And that cost Darth Vader a hand. Still not happy about it. . .

Dixxon-mansionland

Dixxon wakes up and the cats try to tell her about Auntie. Meanwhile Broom seems to be sticking much closer to Auntie Maxx.

"But why would Auntie Maxx want to kill me?"
"Because . . . because . . . because you're the last white witch! And at the next blue moon—in one day—you have to save witchcraft!"

White Cat says, "I'm your friend and fairy godmother, and I've been watching and protecting you for your whole life. And the wolves are sure to kill Bane—the outcast boy who saved you—when he returns to the forest without you."

Second plot point: Dixxon finds out that she's the last

white witch and that White Cat is her fairy god-witch. And that Magnolia, White Cat, cut a deal with Bane to let them kill her so he, Bane, and she could save Dixxon.

Bam!

While our reader may have seen some things coming, for our hero the second plot point is a world changer. Dixxon is informed that she carries the responsibility for the future of magic and mankind. And the fact that her friend Magnolia is now White Cat and not dead? And that cute outcast boy that she kinda liked, but then hated because she thought he killed her friend. . . His pack's gonna kill him for saving her life . . . twice.

PART 4 - WHY DO I APPLAUD?

PURPOSE OF PART 4

The purpose of Part 4 of your novel is none other than to finally give your reader the satisfying ending that we all want.

That means your hero gets everything they ever wanted from their quest, they're martyred as a semi-satisfying twist, or they barely survive and escape in order to fight another day. It's all largely up to you. All those endings find their places in some of the most popular stories today.

WISK

"They call it a Hollywood ending for a reason."

The movie industry knows what a satisfying ending looks like. At least, they know what readers and viewers love, because giving a hero everything they want at the end is how they give a reader or viewer that satisfying feeling inside. That's entertainment—candy.

In our little story, since we're writing a series, we'll solve just enough to make our readers happy, but leave some evil and loose ends to tie up in a future book.

HERO ACCEPTS REALITY

As the last white witch, Dixxon realizes she has responsibility, yet she's still reluctant. Cats tell her that Bane has saved her not once, but three times. When she realizes that the wolf isn't as bad as she thought. . .

"What will happen to him?"
"The pack will banish him . . . or kill him."

Forestland

Dixxon goes to find Bane in the forest to save him from his pack. Along the way, the frogs warn that Bane has been captured by the town's priest and is staked to the witch-burning post, shot through the shoulder with a silver crossbow bolt.

Dixxon tries to save him and gets captured by the evil priest Father Felixx.

It's almost the full blue moon—Dixxon's birthday—and she'll be 16 and all-powerful.

Auntie Maxx shows up and tells Father Felixx that they have to kill Dixxon before she turns into the white witch.

Black and White Cat show up to help. Auntie Maxx is too powerful and she and the priest capture the cats, too.

As the priest and the townspeople are about to burn the "cats," Dixxon's power increases and she escapes.

Priest and Auntie threaten to kill the cats and Bane if Dixxon doesn't surrender. She surrenders.

Dixxon saves Bane by sacrificing herself to Auntie Maxx and Father Felixx. And *that's* how you become a white witch—sacrifice on a blue moon.

Priest lets the cats go and takes Dixxon prisoner, but Auntie takes her from him.

Bane and cats escape into the forest.

Auntie drags Dixxon back to the Mansion to gloat and monologue. (I'll say it again—if villains would just dispatch the heroes when they have the chance, no hero would ever survive Part 3.)

CLIMAX BATTLE SCENE

Mansionland

In the Mangy Mansion kitchen, Auntie taunts Dixxon, gloating and—oh, what's in this cauldron?

Dixxon makes up a lie about the potion. It's the "white witch" brew that brings eternal youth and immortality.

"Youth is wasted on the young," says Auntie Maxx. "And it won't save you, Dixxon, last white witch indeed." Auntie Maxx sips from the cauldron.

Choke-choke Auntie melts down to goo and bursts into purple flame!

NEW EQUILIBRIUM

This is your hero's ride into the sunset moment. She or he has defeated the bad guys, saved the day, and now prepares to live in their new life, happily ever after.

If, however, you're writing a series, this is a short-lived sunset and you have to set up the next installment in the series. Leaving a little mystery at the end does that.

Dixxonland

Black Cat and White Cat and Dixxon and Broom are in the kitchen. Broom is acting strangely.

We flash back to the battle with the townspeople

One of the Witch Council assassins went into the mansion while everyone was gone and hexed Broom.

Not knowing this, Dixxon has resurrected Broom to her own future peril.

Townland

In town, the priest goes through the evil auntie's belongings and finds a locket with a picture of his wife. Evil auntie was the witch who killed his wife all those years ago! In the locket there's a picture of a baby hidden behind the picture of his wife. Hmmm. . .

Forestland

Bane becomes lone wolf and we see the pack chasing him through the forest as we close the scene and the book.

End . . . scene and story!

14
NEXT STEPS

CONGRATULATIONS!

You've just been "lightsabered" senseless with Four Part Story Structure outlining . . . and you survived.

If you follow the advice I've laid out in this book, I have no doubt it will help you outline a relatable and readable story before you ever start writing.

I wrote this book because I wanted to share what I've learned while outlining my own stories and writing to the Four Part Story Structure.

By learning how to walk my heroes through the plot milestones in their stories, I've minimized the time it takes me to write, made editing less time-consuming and learned to publish my novels much faster.

Take the next step.

The key is to take action. Commit to your novel and your goal of becoming a fiction author. Decide today that you'll do everything in your power to learn the mechanics of storytelling.

There's a little gem in everything.

At the beginning of this book I told you that my "methods" wouldn't matter to you, and that's true. You don't have to do things exactly as I do. In fact, you shouldn't.

However, everything we read as fiction writers helps us learn and grow and improve our writing and technique. I truly believe that every book has at least one gem that we walk away with that we wouldn't have found on our own. I know I've tried to pour as many of those nuggets of hard-won wisdom into this book as I possibly could.

I bet that the very next time you sit down to outline a novel, this book will have helped you organize your thoughts and ideas into an easier to follow and more efficient structure.

Take the pieces of this book that resonated with you and use them to help you tell your stories!

But, more importantly, learn all you can—learn what works for you. Then. . .

Do What Works!

JOIN ME

I encourage you to follow my progress as a fiction author and get access to awesome tools and how-to guides to use on your own author journey. In addition, *Dixxon-Teen Witch* (the outlining example novella from this book) will be available in 2015.

To get notified when *Dixxon* is finished, so you can see the final product of our outlining exercise, you can follow me at Vixen Ink, HERE. You can also visit vixenink.com and subscribe to author updates.

You can reach me here:
Email: steve@vixenink.com

The *Nine Day Novel series* starts with this book on outlining for fiction writers.

Other author how-to books in the *Nine Day Novel* series:

9 Day Novel: Outlining
9 Day Novel: Writing
9 Day Novel: Self-Editing
9 Day Novel: Self-Publishing
9 Day Novel: Book Marketing
9 Day Novel: Writing a Series

AUTHOR COACHING

Does it seem like it's taken your entire life to get your first novel out of your dreams and onto the page?

If you're like me, it took you forever to get up the courage to start writing. My first novel took me 27 years to write. I made every mistake a first-time author can make, but *you* don't have to.

After writing 7 novels and publishing 4 of them, now I write faster, with more confidence and greater purpose than I ever have. They laughed at me when I said I would do it, but the draft of my fourth novel took me literally 9 days.

I believe in the power of writing. That's why I'm committed to helping first-time authors get their drafts out of their heads and into readers hands with as little time and struggle as possible.

I'll help you master the three things you have to as a fiction author:

1. Overcoming the belief that you're not "allowed" or "good enough" to write.
2. Learning the mechanics and structure of fiction storytelling.
3. Navigating the technological environment of writing, editing, packaging and physically publishing your first novel.

If you're tired of "aspiring" to become an author and are ready to finally publish your first book, contact me and let's get started!

Email: steve@vixenink.com

15
ABOUT THE AUTHOR

ABOUT THE AUTHOR

Steve Windsor was born in Augsburg, Germany to U.S. military parents. So he doesn't know a bit of German.

I'm just a guy who decided to write one day. And roughly two years and two million words into it, I've learned so much and my writing has improved so much. . . But it all came at a cost in time and frustration. I've bled words.

One of the things I related to a recent interviewer was that if you find the thing that will make you deny sleep, food, bathroom breaks, even sex . . . then that is your true calling. Mine is to write and help other authors overcome their fears and grow their writing "muscle."

My belief is that I have information you need to avoid some of the frustration and pain that I suffered in starting up my dream. And simply put, I want to write books for you because of it.

The fiction I write is hard and raw and my non-fiction is even harder. I don't like to mince words.

I like heroes and villains just about the same, because a good villain usually has a bad backstory that isn't really his or her fault. Sure you gotta kill them, but realize you're going to be a little sad about it, too.

Andrew Vachss is my hero. You should definitely read his novels. And I love George RR Martin because he's not afraid to kill a hero.

I'm here to help you grow as an author. The best way you can do that—go write something!

— Steve Windsor
Best-Selling Author & Writing Coach

I NEED YOUR HELP!

Thank you for reading this book!
I'd love to get your input so I can make the next book in the Nine Day Novel series even better.

I'll have my personal chauffeur, Novella, drive you over to Amazon so you can leave a constructive review, letting me know what you thought of the book. Click HERE and fasten your seatbelt. She's a wild driver!

Thanks so much!
Steve

Made in United States
North Haven, CT
03 December 2023